CROCHET BEYOND THE BASICS

Rita Weiss and Susan Lowman

Leisure Arts, Inc.
Maumelle, Arkansas

Produced by

Production Team

Creative Directors: Jean Leinhauser and
Rita Weiss

Pattern Testers: Sharon Blosch, Karen Blumberg,
Amy Curtin, Susan Jeffers,
Nanette Seale

Book Design: April McArthur

Diagrams © 2014 by The Creative Partners™LLC
Reproduced by special permission

We have made every effort to ensure that these
instructions are accurate and complete. We cannot,
however, be responsible for human error, typographical
mistakes or variations in individual work

Published by Leisure Arts, Inc.
© 2014 by Leisure Arts, Inc.
104 Champs Boulevard, STE. 100
Maumelle, AR 72113
www. leisurearts.com

Library of Congress Control Number: 2014939554

ISBN: 978-1-4647-1551-8

CONTENTS

INTRODUCTION

Have you have been crocheting for a long time, only to find yourself only making granny square afghans? Are you so bored with the same old patterns that you are ready to throw away your crochet hooks and your yarn stash and take up a new hobby?

Instead of throwing away your hooks and your yarn, get them ready for a new adventure. Let's go beyond the basics, and learn crochet techniques from all over the world. Let's go around the world and learn how crochet is worked in other countries. If you yearn for a new kind of crochet, you have come to the right place.

It's great that you know all the basics of crochet. Now is the time to go beyond the basics into a new world of interesting techniques and great patterns. Learn about a technique for making a copy of bobbin lace from a city in Belgium. Recreate the crochet that saved Ireland from the great famine. Find a technique that originated in Poland as a symbol of hope. Make some beautiful lace using a technique that began as a method for creating lace with thread and hairpins.

For each new technique you'll be tackling, we've given you patterns to practice your new skill and to increase your crochet experience.

So keep the crochet hooks and the yarn stash; bury the frustrations of the past, and throw away your feeling that crochet was boring. Get started on learning all about doing crochet beyond the basics.

I know you'll have a rich experience as well as have fun!

-Rita Weiss

BRUGES LACE CROCHET

Bruges Lace Crochet was originally developed as a method of imitating bobbin lace, which required not only huge amounts of equipment, such as wooden bobbins, a special round pillow, thin metal pins and complex patterns but lengthy training and experience as well. The city of Bruges in Belgium became known for a bobbin lace of a scrolling character, and the lace makers in Bruges produced laces which involved creating braids, motif and net patterns and joining them to create specific designs.

Some clever crocheters, looking at the lace produced in Bruges, were able to produce a faster and simpler method of producing a similar lace. Bruges Lace today resembles the original bobbin lace made in Bruges, incorporating the same design elements, but it is created with a crochet hook.

How To Do Bruges Lace Crochet

In Bruges Lace Crochet, lengths of narrow crochet "tapes" are worked in double crochet with turning chains of 5 to 7 stitches that form side loops (also known as chain spaces or arches). These side loops are then joined with crochet into the desired pattern, either while the tape is being formed (to create curves), while another tape is being formed or afterward. Many variations of the tape can also be made with different numbers of stitches, heights of stitches, types of stitches and number of turning chains.

Step 1
Ch 10, dc in 6th ch from hook and in each rem ch across: 5 dc; ch 5, turn.

Step 2
Skip 5 chs, dc in each dc across; ch 5, turn.

Step 3
Repeat Step 2 for desired length of tape. At end of last row, do not ch or turn. Finish off.

Curving Bruges Lace Tapes
Bruges Lace tapes are curved (or shaped) by joining several chain spaces along the same side of the tape to form curves. Anywhere between loose and tight curves can be formed, depending on how many chain spaces a joined. This is usually done by working one slip stitch through a specified number of chain spaces.

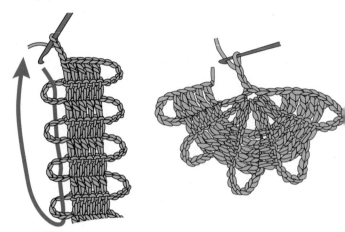

Joining Bruges Lace Tapes
A simple way to join Bruges Lace tapes side by side (either with the same tape or another tape) is to substitu the middle chain of the chain space on the side of the ta with a sl st, sc, dc or taller stitch worked into the chain space of the adjacent tape section.

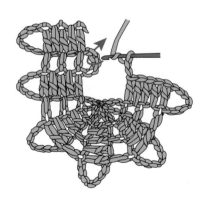

ill Level: Intermediate ■■■□

nished Size: 10" (25.4 cm) diameter

aterials:

ton crochet thread, size 10

0% cotton, 350 yards (320 meters)] per ball

ball light pink (A)

ball white (B)

te: *Photographed model made with Aunt Lydia's* ®
ssic Crochet Thread, size 10 in #401 Orchid Pink and
1 White.

e 7 (1.65mm) steel crochet hook or size required for
auge

ch markers

auge: Rows 1-5 = ¾" (1.91 cm) wide x 1⅛" (2.86
high

Stitch Guide

Double crochet decrease (dc dec): [YO, insert hook in
next st and draw up a loop, YO and draw through 2 lps
on hook] twice, YO and draw through all 3 lps on hook:
dc dec made.

Picot: Ch 3, sl st in top of last st made before ch-3: picot
made.

Note: *To join with sc, make slip knot and place on hook.
Insert hook in indicated st and draw up a lp, YO and
draw through both lps on hook.*

Instructions

Bruges Lace Tape

Row 1 (right side): With A, ch 9, dc in 6th ch from hook,
dc in next 3 chs; ch 5, turn: 4 dc.

Instructions continued on page 6

5

Rows 2 through 4: Dc in first dc and in next 3 sts; ch 5, turn.

Row 5: Dc in first 2 dc, dc dec in next 2 dc; ch 5, turn: 3 dc.

Rows 6 through 10: Dc in first dc and in next 2 sts; ch 5, turn.

Row 11: Dc in first dc and in next 2 sts; ch 2, insert hook in previous 3 ch-5 sps on same edge of tape and work 1 sc through all 3 sps at once, ch 2, turn.

Row 12: Rep Row 6.

Row 13: Dc in first 2 dc, 2 dc in last dc; ch 2, dc in ch-5 sp at end of Row 3, ch 2, turn: 4 dc.

Row 14: Rep Row 2.

Row 15: Dc in first dc and in next 3 sts; ch 2, dtr in ch-5 sp at end of Row 1, ch 2, turn.

Rows 16 and 17: Rep Row 2, twice.

Row 18: Work 2 dc in first dc, dc in next 3 sts; ch 5, turn: 5 dc.

Rows 19 through 25: Dc in first dc and in next 4 sts; ch 5, turn.

Row 26: Dc in first dc and in next 4 sts; ch 2, insert hook in previous 3 ch-3 sps on same edge of tape and work 1 sc through all 3 sps at once, ch 2, turn.

Row 27: Dc in first 4 dc, 2 dc in last dc; ch 5, turn: 6 dc.

Row 28: Work 2 dc in first dc, dc in next 5 sts; ch 5, turn: 7 dc.

Row 29: Dc in first dc and in next 6 sts; ch 5, turn.

Row 30: Dc dec in first 2 dc, dc in next 5 sts; ch 5, turn: 6 dc. Place marker in ch-5 sp at beg of row.

Row 31: Dc in first 4 dc, dc dec in last 2 dc; ch 5, turn: 5 dc.

Rows 32 through 35: Rep Row 19, 4 times.

Row 36: Dc in first dc and in next 4 sts; ch 2, insert hook

in previous 3 ch-3 sps on same edge of tape and work 1 through all 3 sps at once, ch 3, turn.

Rows 37 through 39: Rep Row 18, 3 times.

Row 40: Dc dec in first 2 dc, dc in next 3 sts; ch 2, dtr ch-5 sp at end of Row 16, ch 2, turn: 4 dc.

Row 41: Rep Row 2.

Row 42: Dc in first dc and in next 3 sts; ch 2, tr in ch-5 at end of Row 14, ch 2, turn.

Row 43: Rep Row 2.

Row 44: Dc in first dc and in next 3 sts; ch 2, dc in ch-3 sp at end of Row 12, ch 2, turn.

Row 45: Dc in first 2 dc, dc dec in last 2 sts; ch 5, turn: dc.

Row 46: Dc in first dc and in next 2 sts; ch 2, sc in ch-5 sp at end of Row 10, ch 2, turn.

Rows 47 through 206: Rep Rows 7 through 46, 4 time joining to repeats of specified rows.

Rows 207 through 209: Rep Rows 7 through 9.

Row 210: Dc in first dc and in next 2 sts; ch 2, sc in ch-sp at end of Row 6, ch 2, turn.

Row 211: Rep Row 11.

Row 212: Dc in first dc and in next 2 sts; ch 2, dc in ch-sp at end of Row 4, ch 2, turn.

Row 213: Rep Row 13.

Row 214: Dc in first dc and in next 3 sts; ch 2, tr in ch-sp at end of Row 2, ch 2, turn.

Row 215: Rep Row 15.

Row 216: Dc in first dc and in next 3 sts; ch 2, dtr in ch-sp at beg of Row 1, ch 2, turn.

Rows 217 through 240: Rep Rows 17 through 40: 6 curved points. Finish off. Whip stitch chs at base of 4 s on Row 1 to top of 4 sts on last row. Weave in ends.

-In Sections

nter Motif

d 1 (right side): With B, ch 4, join with sl st to form a
, ch 1, [sc in ring, ch 5] 5 times, sc in ring; join with
, dc in first sc (ch 2 and dc counts as last ch-5 sp): 5
5 sps.

d 2: Ch 1, sc around post of joining dc, ch 3, with right
facing, sc in any ch-5 sp at center of Bruges Lace,
, [sc in next ch-5 sp on Center Motif, ch 3, sc in next
5 sp at center of Bruges Lace, ch 3] 5 times; join with
in first sc. Finish off; weave in ends.

ter Motifs (work on each of 6 Bruges Lace
er curved points)

h right side facing and B, ch 4, join with sl st to form a
; ch 1, sc in ring, ch 3, sc in ch-5 sp at end of Row 18,
, sc in ring, ch 4, sc around post of joining dtr, ch 4, sc
ing, ch 3, sc in ch-5 sp at end of Row 38 (row before
ing dtr), ch 3, sc in ring, ch 4, sc in inner curve joining

of Row 36, ch 4, sc in ring, ch 3, sc in ch-5 sp at end of
Row 28, ch 3, sc in ring, ch 4, sc in inner curve joining of
Row 26, ch 4; join with sl st in first sc. Finish off; weave
in ends.

Edging

Rnd 1 (right side): With right side facing, join B with sc
in marked ch-5 sp; *[ch 7, sc in next ch-5 sp] 6 times, ch
3, sc around post of dtr, ch 3, sc in next ch-5 sp, ch 3, sc
in last ch-7 sp made, ch 3, sc in next ch-5 sp, ch 3, dc in
next ch-7 sp, ch 3, [sc in next ch-5 sp, ch 7] 3 times**; sc
in next ch-5 sp; rep from * around, ending last rep at **;
join with sl st in first sc.

Rnd 2: Ch 1, sc in same st as joining; *[(4 sc, picot, 3 sc)
in next ch-7 sp, sc in next sc] 4 times, 3 sc in next ch-7 sp,
sc around post of next dc, 3 sc in next ch-7 sp, [sc in next
sc, (4 sc, picot, 3 sc) in next ch-7 sp] 3 times**; sc in next
sc; rep from * around, ending last rep at **; join with sl st
in first sc: 42 picots. Finish off; weave in ends.

Wash and block.

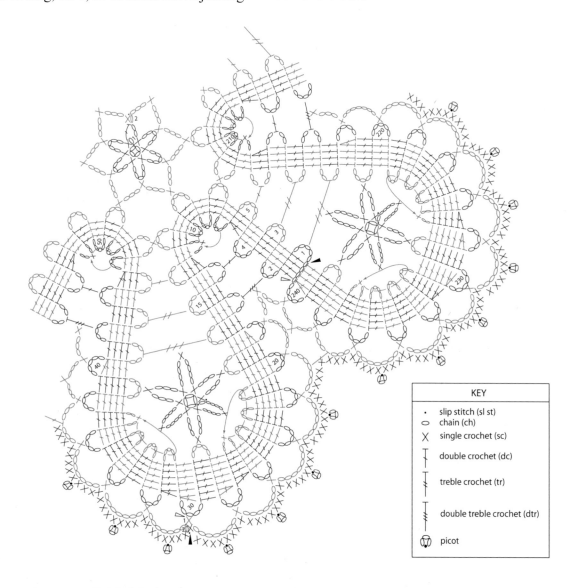

KEY	
·	slip stitch (sl st)
o	chain (ch)
X	single crochet (sc)
⊤	double crochet (dc)
⊤	treble crochet (tr)
⊤	double treble crochet (dtr)
⊕	picot

Bruges Lace Heart Centerpiece

Designed by Susan Lowman

ill Level: Intermediate ■■ ■ □

nished Size: 22" (56 cm) diameter

aterials:
e 10 Crochet thread

[100% cotton, 350 yards (320 meters)] per ball
 ball red (A)
0 yds light pink (C)
0 yds medium pink (D)
[100% cotton, 400 yards (365 meters)] per ball
 ball white (B)
[% cotton/12% metallic, 100 yards (91.4 meters)] per
 all
 mall amount white/silver (E)

te: Photographed model made with Aunt Lydia's®
assic Crochet Thread, size 10 #494 Victory Red, #1
ite, #401 Orchid Pink, #493 French Rose and Aunt
dia's® Metallic Crochet Thread, size 10 #1S White/
ver.

e 7 (1.65 mm) steel crochet hook (or size required for
auge)
tch markers

auge: Rows First center heart = 3½" (8.89 cm) wide x
" (6.99 cm) high

itch Guide

tended double crochet (edc): YO, insert hook in
·cified st and draw up a loop, YO and draw through one
 on hook, [YO and draw through 2 lps on hook] twice:
 made.

structions

nter Hearts (make 4)

te: First and 2nd hearts will be right side up. Third
d 4th hearts will be wrong side up.

rst Heart

w 1 (right side): With A, ch 9, dc in 6th ch from hook,
 in next 3 chs; ch 5, turn: 4 dc.

ws 2 through 5: Dc in first dc and in next 3 sts; ch 5, turn.

w 6: Dc in first 2 dc, hdc in next st, sc in next st; ch 1,
n: 4 sts.

w 7: Sc in next sc, hdc in next hdc, dc in next 2 dc; ch
 turn.

Rows 8 and 9: Rep Rows 6 and 7. Place marker in ch-5
sp at end of Row 9.

Row 10: Dc in first st and in next 3 sts; ch 1, turn.

Row 11: Sc in first st, hdc in next st, dc in next 2 sts; ch 5,
turn.

Row 12: Dc in first 2 dc, hdc in next hdc, sc in next sc; ch
1, turn.

Row 13: Rep Row 11.

Row 14: Dc in first 2 dc, hdc in next hdc, sc in next sc; ch
5, turn.

Rows 15 through 24: Rep Rows 10 through 14, twice.

Row 25: Dc in first sc, dc in next 3 sts; ch 5, turn.

Rows 26 through 29: Rep Rows 6 through 9.

Rows 30 through 35: Rep Row 2, 6 times.

Rows 36 through 39: Rep Rows 6 through 9.

Row 40: Dc in first dc and in next 3 sts. Finish off. Whip
stitch chs at base of 4 sts on Row 1 to top of 4 sts on Row
40. Weave in ends.

2nd Heart
Make same as First Heart.

3rd Heart

Row 1 (wrong side): With A, ch 9, dc in 6th ch from
hook, dc in next 3 chs, ch 2; sc in ch-5 sp at end of Row 1
on First Heart, ch 2, turn: 4 dc.

Row 2: Rep Row 2 on First Heart.

Row 3: Dc in first dc and in next 3 sts; ch 2, sc in ch-5 sp
at end of Row 3 on First Heart, ch 2, turn.

Row 4: Rep Row 2 on First Heart.

Row 5: Dc in first dc and in next 3 sts; ch 2, sc in ch-5 sp
at end of Row 5 on First Heart, ch 2, turn.

Rows 6 through 26: Rep Rows 6 through 26 on First
Heart.

Instructions continued on page 10

Row 27: Sc in next sc, hdc in next hdc, dc in next 2 dc; ch 2, sc in ch-5 sp at end of Row 27 on 2nd Heart, ch 2, turn: 4 sts.

Row 28: Rep Row 6 on First Heart.

Row 29: Sc in next sc, hdc in next hdc, dc in next 2 dc; ch 2, sc in ch-5 sp at end of Row 29 on 2nd Heart, ch 2, turn.

Row 30: Rep Row 2 on First Heart.

Row 31: Dc in first dc and in next 3 sts; ch 2, sc in ch-5 sp at end of Row 31 on 2nd Heart, ch 2, turn.

Row 32: Rep Row 2 on First Heart.

Row 33: Dc in first dc and in next 3 sts; ch 2, sc in ch-5 sp at end of Row 33 on 2nd Heart, ch 2, turn.

Row 34: Rep Row 2 on First Heart.

Row 35: Dc in first dc and in next 3 sts; ch 2, sc in ch-5 sp at end of Row 35 on 2nd Heart, ch 2, turn.

Row 36: Rep Row 6 on First Heart.

Row 37: Sc in next sc, hdc in next hdc, dc in next 2 dc; ch 2, sc in ch-5 sp at end of Row 37 on First Heart, ch 2, turn.

Row 38: Rep Row 6 on First Heart.

Row 39: Sc in next sc, hdc in next hdc, dc in next 2 dc; ch 2, sc in ch-5 sp at end of Row 39 on First Heart, ch 2, turn.

Row 40: Rep Row 40 on First Heart.

4th Heart

Make same as 3rd Heart, working joining sc on Rows 1, 3, 5, 37 and 39 to 2nd Heart and Rows 27, 29, 31, 33 and 35 to First Heart.

Outer Hearts

First Heart

Row 1 (wrong side): With A, ch 9, dc in 6th ch from hook, dc in next 3 chs; ch 5, turn: 4 dc.

Rows 2 through 14: Dc in first dc and in next 3 sts; ch 5, turn. Place marker in ch-5 sp at end of Rows 2, 5, 9 and 1

Row 15: Dc in first 2 dc, hdc in next st, sc in next st; ch turn: 4 sts.

Row 16: Sc in next sc, hdc in next hdc, dc in next 2 dc; c 5, turn. Place marker in ch-5 sp.

Rows 17 and 18: Rep Rows 15 and 16.

Row 19 and 20: Rep Row 2, twice.

Rows 21 through 24: Rep Rows 15 through 18.

Rows 25 through 34: Rep Row 2, 10 times. Place mark in ch-5 sp at end of Rows 28 and 31.

Rows 35 through 40: Rep Rows 15 and 16, 3 times. Place marker in ch-5 sp at end of Row 38.

Rows 41 and 42: Rep Row 2, twice.

Row 43: Dc in first dc and in next 3 sts; ch 2, sc in marked ch-5 sp at end of Row 5, ch 2, turn. Remove marker.

Rows 44 and 45: Rep Row 2, twice, working in front of previous lace rows.

Row 46: Dc in first dc and in next 3 sts; ch 2, sc in marked ch-5 sp at end of Row 2, ch 2, turn. Remove marker.

Rows 47 through 50: Rep Row 2, 4 times.

Rows 51 through 60: Rep Rows 15 through 24. Place marker in ch-5 sp at end of Row 56.

Row 61: Rep Row 2.

Row 62: Dc in first dc and in next 3 sts; ch 2, sc in marked ch-5 sp at end of Row 12, ch 2, turn. Remove marker.

Rows 63 and 64: Rep Row 2, twice, working behind previous lace rows.

Row 65: Dc in first dc and in next 3 sts; ch 2, sc in marked ch-5 sp at end of Row 9, ch 2, turn. Remove marker.

...s 66 through 68: Rep Row 2, 3 times.

...69: Dc in first dc and in next 3 sts; ch 2, sc in ...ked ch-5 sp at end of Row 31, ch 2, turn. Remove ...ker.

...s 70 and 71: Rep Row 2, twice, working in front of ...ious lace rows.

...72: Dc in first dc and in next 3 sts; ch 2, sc in ...ked ch-5 sp at end of Row 28, ch 2, turn. Remove ...ker.

...s 73 through 75: Rep Row 2, 3 times.

...s 76 and 77: Rep Rows 15 and 16.

...78: Dc in first 2 dc, hdc in next hdc, sc in next sc; ch ...rn.

...d through 8th Hearts

...1: With A, dc in next sc and in next 3 sts; ch 5, turn: ...

...s 2 through 78: Rep Rows 2 through 78 on First ...rt. At end of 8th Heart, do not ch 5. Finish off. ...move tail from center of hearts. Whip stitch top of sts ...Row 78 of 8th Heart to chs at base of 4 sts on Row 1 of ...t Heart. Weave in all ends.

...er Small Circle

...1 (wrong side): With B, ch 9, dc in 6th ch from hook ... in next 3 chs; ch 2, sc in marked ch-5 sp at end of ...9 of First Heart, ch 2, turn: 4 dc.

...2: Dc in first dc and in next 3 sts; ch 5, turn.

...3: Dc in first dc and in next 3 sts; ch 2, sc in next ...5 sp on same heart, ch 2, turn: 4 sts.

...4: Rep Row 2.

...5: Dc in first dc and in next 3 sts; ch 1, turn.

...6: Sc in first dc, hdc in next dc, dc in next 2 dc; ch 5, ...n.

...s 7 through 10: Rep Row 2, 4 times.

...s 11 and 12: Rep Rows 5 and 6.

Row 13: Dc in first dc and in next 3 sts; ch 2, sk 2 ch-5 sps on same heart, sc in next ch-5 sp on same heart, ch 2, turn.

Rows 14 through 24: Rep Rows 2 through 12.

Row 25: Dc in first dc and in next 3 sts; ch 2, sk last ch-5 sp on same heart and first ch-5 sp on next heart, sc in next ch-5 sp on next heart, ch 2, turn.

Rows 26 through 73: Rep Rows 2 through 25, twice.

Rows 74 through 95: Rep Rows 2 through 23.

Row 96: Sc in first dc, hdc in next dc, dc in next 2 dc. Finish off. Whip stitch chs at base of 4 sts on Row 1 to top of 4 sts on Row 96. Weave in ends.

Outer Small Circle

Row 1 (wrong side): With B, ch 9, edc in 6th ch from hook, edc in next ch, dc in next 2 chs; ch 2, sc in ch-5 sp at beg of Row 1 of Inner Circle, ch 2, turn.

Row 2: Dc in first 2 dc, edc in next 2 edc; ch 5, turn.

Row 3: Edc in first 2 edc, dc in next 2 dc; ch 2, sc in next ch-5 sp on outer edge of Inner Circle, ch 2, turn.

Rows 4 through 7: Rep Rows 2 and 3, twice.

Row 8: Dc in first 2 dc, edc in next 2 edc; ch 2, sc in marked ch-5 sp at end of Row 38 on any heart on Outer Hearts, ch 2, turn.

Row 9: Rep Row 3.

Row 10: Dc in first 2 dc, edc in next 2 edc; ch 2, sc in ch-5 sp at end of Row 36 on same heart on Outer Hearts, ch 2, turn.

Row 11: Rep Row 3.

Rows 12 through 19: Rep Rows 2 and 3, 4 times.

Row 20: Dc in first 2 dc, edc in next 2 edc; ch 2, sc in marked ch-5 sp at end of Row 38 on next heart on Outer Hearts, ch 2, turn.

Rows 21 through 92: Rep Rows 9 through 20, 6 times.

Instructions continued on page 12

Rows 93 through 95: Rep Rows 9 through 11.

Row 96: Dc in first 2 dc, edc in next 2 edc. Finish off. Whip stitch chs at base of 4 sts on Row 1 to top of 4 sts on Row 96. Weave in ends.

Inner Large Circle

Row 1 (wrong side): With B, ch 9, dc in 6th ch from hook, dc in next 3 chs; ch 5, turn: 4 dc.

Row 2: Dc in first 2 dc, edc in next 2 dc; ch 5, turn.

Row 3: Dc in first 2 edc, dc in next 2 dc; ch 5, turn.

Rows 4 through 11: Rep Rows 2 and 3, 4 times.

Row 12: Rep Row 2.

Row 13: Dc in first 2 edc, dc in next 2 dc; ch 2, sc in marked ch-5 sp at end of Row 56 on any Outer Heart, ch 2, turn.

Row 14: Rep Row 2.

Row 15: Dc in first 2 edc, dc in next 2 dc; ch 2, sc in ch-5 sp at end of Row 58 on same Outer Heart, ch 2, turn.

Rows 16 through 21: Rep Rows 2 and 3, 3 times

Row 22: Rep Row 2.

Row 23: Dc in first 2 edc, dc in next 2 dc; ch 2, sc in marked ch-5 sp at end of Row 16 on same Outer Heart, ch 2, turn.

Row 24: Rep Row 2.

Row 25: Dc in first 2 edc, dc in next 2 dc; ch 2, sc in ch-5 sp at end of Row 18 on same Outer Heart, ch 2, turn.

Rows 26 through 39: Rep Rows 2 and 3, 7 times.

Row 40: Rep Row 2.

Row 41: Dc in first 2 edc, dc in next 2 dc; ch 2, sc in marked ch-5 sp at end of Row 56 on next Outer Heart, ch 2, turn.

Rows 42 through 209: Rep Rows 14 through 41, 6 times.

Rows 210 through 223: Rep Rows 14 through 27.

Row 224: Dc in first 2 dc, edc in next 2 dc. Finish off. Whip stitch chs at base of 4 sts on Row 1 to top of 4 sts on Row 224. Weave in ends.

Outer Large Circle

Row 1 (wrong side): With B, ch 9, edc in 6th ch from hook and in next 3 chs; ch 2, sc in ch-5 sp at beg of Row 1 on Inner Large Circle, ch 2, turn: 4 sts.

Row 2: Dc in first 2 edc, edc in next 2 edc; ch 5, turn.

Row 3: Edc in first 2 edc, edc in next 2 dc; ch 2, sc in next ch-5 sp on outer edge of Inner Large Circle, ch 2, turn.

Rows 4 through 223: Rep Rows 2 and 3, 110 times.

Row 224: Dc in first 2 edc, edc in next 2 edc. Finish off. Whip stitch chs at base of 4 sts on Row 1 to top of 4 sts on Row 224. Weave in ends.

Fill-In Sections

Section 1 (work in each of 8 open spaces between Outer Small Circle and Outer Hearts)

Rnd 1 (right side): With C, ch 5, join with sl st to form ring, ch 5 (counts as dc and ch-2 sp), sc in ch-5 sp at end of any Row 77 of Outer Hearts (rows between hearts), 2, dc in ring, ch 2, sc in next ch-5 sp of Outer Hearts (a end of Row 75), ch 2, dc in ring, ch 5, sc in ch-5 sp at e of Row 32 of next heart on Outer Hearts, ch 5, dc in rin ch 6, sc in next ch-5 sp of same heart on Outer Hearts (end of Row 34), ch 7, dc in ring, ch 3, sc in 2nd unjoined ch-5 sp of Outer Small Circle (of 4 unjoined ch-5 sps between Outer Hearts), ch 3, dc in ring, ch 3, sc in 3rd unjoined ch-5 sp of Outer Small Circle, ch 3, dc in ring ch 7, sc in ch-5 sp at end of Row 40 of next Outer Hear ch 6, dc in ring, ch 5, sc in next ch-5 sp of same Outer Heart (at end of Row 42), ch 5; join with sl st in 3rd ch o beg ch-5: 8 dc and 8 spokes. Finish off; weave in ends.

Section 2 (work in each of 8 open spaces between In Large Circle and Outer Hearts)

Rnd 1 (right side): With D, ch 5, join with sl st to form a ring, ch 10 (counts as tr and ch-6 sp), sc in 3rd unjoined ch-5 sp of Inner Large Circle (of 7 unjoined ch-5 sps

ween Outer Hearts), ch 5, tr in ring, ch 5, sk next ch-5
on Inner Large Circle, sc in next ch-5 sp on Inner Large
cle, ch 6, tr in ring, ch 3, sc in ch-5 sp at end of Row 24
next heart on Outer Hearts, ch 2, tr in ring, ch 2, sc in
t ch-5 sp on same heart of Outer Hearts (at end of Row
, ch 3, tr in ring, ch 6, sc in ch-5 sp at end of Row 74 of
er Hearts, ch 5, tr in ring, ch 5, sc in ch-5 sp at beg of
w 1 of next Outer Heart, ch 6, tr in ring, ch 3, sc in ch-5
t end of Row 48 of same Outer Heart, ch 2, tr in ring,
2, sc in next ch-5 sp of same outer Heart (at end of row
, ch 3; join with sl st in 4ᵗʰ ch of beg ch-10: 8 tr and 8
kes. Finish off; weave in ends.

Section 3 (work in each of 4 open center spaces of Inner Hearts)

Rnd 1: With wrong side facing on 1ˢᵗ and 2ⁿᵈ Hearts or right side facing on 3ʳᵈ and 4ᵗʰ Hearts, join E with sc in ch-5 sp at end of Row 4 of any Center Heart, ch 3, sc in ch-5 sp at end of Row 14, ch 3, sc in ch-5 sp at end of Row 2, ch 4, sc in ch-5 sp at end of Row 16, ch 4, sc in ch-5 sp at beg of Row 1, ch 4, sc in ch-5 sp at end of Row 32, ch 4, sc in ch-5 sp at end of Row 16, ch 4, sc in ch-5 sp at end of Row 30, ch 3, sc in ch-5 sp at end of Row 18, ch 3, sc in ch-5 sp at end of Row 24: 10 sc and 9 ch-sps. Finish off; weave in ends.

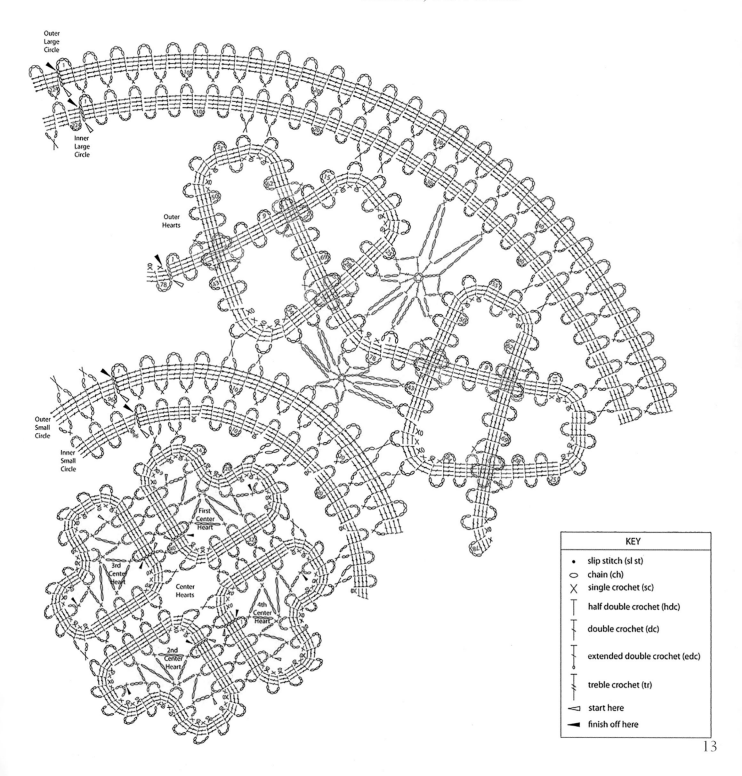

KEY	
•	slip stitch (sl st)
○	chain (ch)
✕	single crochet (sc)
	half double crochet (hdc)
	double crochet (dc)
	extended double crochet (edc)
	treble crochet (tr)
◁	start here
◀	finish off here

13

TUNISIAN CROCHET

Sometimes it's called **Tunisian Crochet** although we have no idea if it came from Tunisia. Sometimes it's called **Afghan Stitch**, but we don't know if it may have originated in Afghanistan, and it's used for more than just making afghans. Sometimes it's called **Tricot Crochet**, tricot being the French word for knitting. That might be because it's worked on a special crochet hook that has a knob on the end like a knitting needle, and at one point in each row all the stitches sit on the hook as they do in knitting.

Unlike regular crochet, Tunisian Crochet is worked in rows which are not turned. The right side is always facing the crocheter. In addition, the loop on the hook is *always* counted as a stitch. The work is done using a long straight hook since at one point in each row all the stitches are on the hook. Each row actually consists of two parts. In Part One all of the loops are placed on the hook. In Part Two all of the loops except for one are removed from the hook. The final result is an almost perfectly square stitch.

How To Do Tunisian Crochet

Foundation Row:
Chain the number specified in the pattern.

Step 1: Skip the first chain from the hook; *insert the hook through the top loop only of the next chain, yarn over and draw the loop through, forming a new loop on the hook (Fig 1).

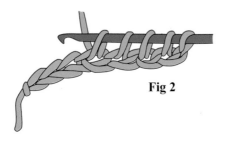

Fig 1

Repeat from * across the chain, keeping all loops on the hook (Fig 2). Do not chain or turn at the end of the row.

Fig 2

Step 2: Yarn over and draw through the first loop on th[e] hook; *yarn over and draw through 2 loops (Fig 3).

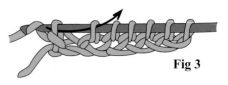

Fig 3

Repeat from * across. At the end, one loop will remain on the hook and is the first stitch of the next row. Do n[ot] chain or turn the work!

Pattern Row:

Step 1: Insert hook in vertical bar of second stitch (Fig 4)

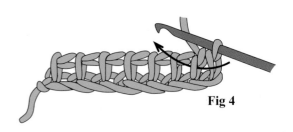

Fig 4

Yarn over and draw through, adding a new loop on the hook; *insert hook in vertical bar of next stitch and dra[w] through, adding a new loop on the hook; repeat from * across to the last vertical bar. For a firmer side edge, on [the] last bar insert hook through both vertical bar and thread behind it and work them together as one (Fig 5).

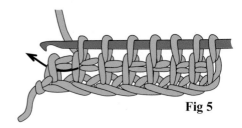

Fig 5

Step 2: Repeat Step 2 of the Foundation Row. Repeat Steps 1 and 2 of the Pattern Row until the piece is the desired length.

Note: *Because the first loop on each row is not a full stitch, there will always be one more loop than the number of stitches shown on the charts for each row.*

Tunisian Bookmark

Designed by Susan Lowman

Skill Level: Easy ■■□□

Finished Size: Approx. 6¾" high x 1½" wide (17.1 cm x 3.8 cm)

Materials:
Sport weight yarn (2 Fine)
[100% cotton, 1.75 ounces, 137 yards (50 grams, 125 meters)] per ball
   1 ball rainbow
Note: *Photographed model made with SMC Catania #82 Rainbow Print.*
Size G/6 (4 mm) afghan hook (or size required for gauge)
Tapestry needle

Gauge:
6 sts = 1" (2.5 cm)
5 rows = 1" (2.5 cm)

Instructions

Row 1 (first half): Ch 7; insert hook in back bar of 2nd ch from hook and draw up a lp; *insert hook in back bar of next ch and draw up a lp; rep from * across: 7 lps on hook.
Row 1 (second half): YO and draw through one lp on hook; *YO and draw through 2 lps on hook; rep from * across until 1 lp rem on hook.

Row 2 (first half): Skip first vertical bar; *insert hook under next vertical bar and draw up a lp; rep from * across: 7 lps on hook.

Row 2 (second half): Rep Row 1 (second half).

Rows 3 through 30: Rep Row 2 (first half and second half) 28 times more.

Bind off row: Skip first vertical bar; *insert hook under next vertical bar and draw up a lp, pull lp through lp on hook (sl st made); rep from * across. Do not finish off.

Edging
Ch 1, sc in edge of each row across side edge; ch 1, sc in free lps of each ch across bottom edge; ch 1, sc in edge of each row across next side edge; ch 1, sc in each sl st across top edge; join with sl st in first sc. Finish off; weave in ends.

Wash and block.

Tunisian Christmas Tree Afghan

Designed by Susan Lowman

Skill Level: Intermediate
■■■□

Finished Size: Approx. 49" x 66"
(124.46 cm x 167.64 cm) plus edging

Materials:
Worsted weight yarn [4] Medium
[100% acrylic, 7 ounces, 364 yards
(198 grams, 333 meters)] per skein
  3 skeins white
  3 skeins green
  3 skeins red
Note: *Photographed model made
with Red Heart® Super Saver® #311
White, #368 Paddy Green and #319
Cherry Red.*
Size J/10 (6 mm) afghan hook or
  double ended crochet hook (or size
  required for gauge)
Size J/10 (6 mm) crochet hook
Tapestry needle

Gauge:
Square with edging = 8¼" wide x 8"
high (20.95 cm x 20.95 cm)
Square before edging = 6¼" wide x
6¼" high (15.875 cm x 15.875 cm)

Stitch Guide

Single crochet decrease (sc dec):
[Insert hook in next st and draw up a
lp] twice; YO and draw through all
lps on hook: sc dec made.

Double crochet decrease (dc dec):
*YO, insert hook in first indicated
st and draw up a lp, YO and draw
through 2 lps on hook; rep from *
in next indicated st; YO and draw
through all 3 lps on hook: dc dec
made.

Beginning cluster (beg CL): Ch
2, dc in same st as joining: beg CL
made.

Cluster (CL): [YO, insert hook in
indicated st and draw up a lp, YO and
draw through 2 lps on hook] twice;
YO and draw through all 3 lps on
hook: CL made.

structions

ite Squares (make 10)

v 1 (first half): With afghan hook and white, ch 22;
rt hook in back bar of 2nd ch from hook and draw up a
*insert hook in back bar of next ch and draw up a lp;
from * across: 22 lps on hook.

v 1 (second half): YO and draw through one lp on
k; *YO and draw through 2 lps on hook; rep from *
oss until 1 lp rem on hook.

v 2 (first half): Skip first vertical bar; *insert hook
er next vertical bar and draw up a lp; rep from *
oss: 22 lps on hook.

v 2 (second half): Rep Row 1 (second half).

vs 3-18: Rep Row 2 (first half and second half) 16
es more.

d off row: Skip first vertical bar; *insert hook under
t vertical bar and draw up a lp, pull lp through lp on
k (sl st made); rep from * across. Finish off; weave in
s.

en Squares (make 9)
h green, work same as White Square.

l Squares (make 8)
h red, work same as White Square.

e Squares (make 8)

v 1 (first and second half): Work same as Rows 1 and
White Square (first and second half).

Rows 2 and 3 (first half): Skip first vertical bar; *insert
hook under next vertical bar and draw up a lp*; rep from
* to * 9 times more; drop white to back and pick up
green, crossing green over white; with green, rep from *
to * once; drop green to back and pick up white, crossing
white over green; with white, rep from * to * 10 times: 21
lps of white and 1 lp of green on hook.

Rows 2 and 3 (second half): With white, YO and draw
through one lp on hook; *YO and draw through 2 lps on
hook*; rep from * to * 8 times more; drop white to back
and pick up green, crossing green over white; with green,
rep from * to * once; drop green to back and pick up
white, crossing white over green; with white, rep from *
to * 11 times: 1 lp of white on hook.

Rows 4 through 18: Work in same manner, changing
colors as per tree chart.

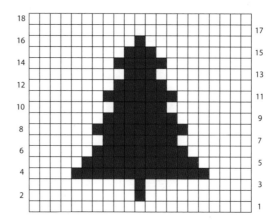

Bind off row: Work same as bind off row on White
Square.

Edging on all squares

Rnd 1: With right side facing and J hook, join green with
sc in first sl st on bind off row, sc in same st, sc in next 19
sl sts on bind off row, 2 sc in last sl st, 2 sc in edge of Row
18, sc in edge of next 16 rows, 2 sc in edge of Row 1, 2
sc in free lps of first ch on foundation ch, sc in free lps of
next 19 chs, 2 sc in free lps of last ch, 2 sc in edge of Row
1, sc in edge of next 16 rows, 2 sc in edge of Row 18; join
with sl st in first sc: 86 sc. Finish off; weave in ends.

Rnd 2: With right side facing and J hook, working in
back lps of each st, join white with sc in first sc on Rnd 1,
sc in same sc; *sc in next 21 sc, 2 sc in each of next 2 sc,
sc in next 18 sc*; 2 sc in each of next 2 sc; rep from * to *
once; 2 sc in next sc; join with sl st in both lps of first sc:
94 sc. Finish off; weave in ends.

Instructions continued on page 18

Rnd 3: With right side facing and J hook, working in back lps of each st, join red with sc in first sc on Rnd 2, sc in same sc; *sc in next 23 sc, 2 sc in each of next 2 sc, sc in next 20 sc*; 2 sc in each of next 2 sc; rep from * to * once; 2 sc in next sc; join with sl st in both lps of first sc: 102 sc. Finish off, leaving a 30" end for sewing. Weave in beginning end.

Assembly

Referring to diagram for placement, join squares together in 7 rows of 5 squares each. To join squares, hold 2 squares with wrong sides together; with tapestry needle and red ends, sew squares together through both loops. Join rows of squares together in same manner, making sure all corners are firmly joined.

Border

Rnd 1: With right side facing and J hook, join red with sc in first sc on Rnd 3 of Edging on top right-hand square, work 2 more sc in same sc; *sc in each sc across to joining of squares, dc dec in next 2 joined sc on current square and next square; rep from * around, working 3 sc in each corner (in 3rd sc of 4 sc in corner at beg of top and bottom edges and in 2nd sc of 4 sc in corner at end of top and bottom edges); join with sl st in first sc.

Rnd 2: Sl st in next sc, ch 1, 3 sc in same sc, sc in each sc around, working 3 sc in each corner and sc dec in center of left and right edges; join with sl st in first sc. Finish off; weave in ends.

Rnd 3: With right side facing and J hook, join green with sc in 2nd sc on Rnd 2 (center sc of corner), work 2 more sc in same sc, sc in each sc around, working 3 sc in center of each corner; join with sl st in first sc.

Rnd 4: Work beg CL, ch 1, (CL, ch 1) in each of next 2 sc; *skip next sc, CL in next sc, ch 1; rep from * across to next corner; skip next sc**; (CL, ch 1) in each of next 3 sc on corner; rep from * around, ending final rep at **; join with sl st in top of beg CL.

Rnd 5: Sl st in next ch-1 sp, ch 4 (counts as first hdc and ch-2 sp); *hdc in next ch-1 sp, ch 1; rep from * around, working (hdc in next ch-1 sp, ch 2) in center of each corner; join with sl st in 2nd ch of beg ch-4.

Rnd 6: Sl st in next ch-2 sp, work beg CL, ch 1, [CL, ch 1] 2 times in same ch-2 sp; *CL in next ch-1 sp, ch 1; rep from * around, working [CL, ch 1] 3 times in each corner ch-2 sp; join with sl st in top of beg CL. Finish off; weave in ends.

Rnd 7: With right side facing and J hook, join white with sl st in first ch-1 sp on Rnd 6, ch 2 (counts as hdc), hdc in same ch-1 sp, ch 1, 2 hdc in center CL, ch 1, 2 hdc in next ch-1 sp, work 2 hdc in each ch-1 sp around, working (2 hdc in next ch-1 sp, ch 1, 2 hdc in center CL, ch 1, 2 hdc in next ch-1 sp) in each corner; join with sl st in 2nd ch of beg ch-2. Finish off; weave in ends.

Rnd 8: With right side facing and J hook, join red with sl st in first ch-1 sp on Rnd 7, ch 3 (counts as dc), dc in same ch-1 sp, ch 1, skip next hdc, (dc, tr, dc) in next hdc, ch 1; *2 dc in sp before next 2 hdc; rep from * around, working [2 dc in sp before next 2 hdc, ch 1, skip next hdc, (dc, tr, dc) in next hdc, ch 1, 2 dc in sp before next 2 hdc] in each corner; join with sl st in 3rd ch of beg ch-3. Finish off; weave in ends.

Rnd 9: With right side facing and J hook, join green with sc in ch of first ch-1 sp on Rnd 8, sc in next dc, work 3 sc in next tr, sc in each st and ch around, working 3 sc in each corner; join with sl st in first sc. Finish off; weave in ends.

BROOMSTICK LACE CROCHET

Broomstick Lace (or Crochet) is an historic technique that is over 100 years old that has a distinctive lacy appearance. It has been called "Jiffy Lace" as well as "Peacock Eye Crochet."

The work was probably originally worked with a crochet hook and an actual broomstick. Today this stitch uses a crochet hook that is suitable for the yarn used as well as a large knitting needle, usually size 35 (19 mm) or 50 (25 mm). In addition several companies now offer Broomstick Lace Needles in various diameters.

As with most crochet, a Broomstick Lace pattern begins with a chain. This chain is normally in multiples of 3 through 6. In our instructions, we show the work done with 15 stitches.

How To Do Broomstick Lace

To start, place a slip knot on the hook and chain 15. Each row will now consist of two parts.

Part One

With knitting needle or broomstick lace needle in the left hand, draw up a loop on the crochet hook and slip it onto the needle. *Insert the hook into the next chain, draw up a long loop and slip it onto the needle; repeat from * across the chain: 15 loops now on the needle.

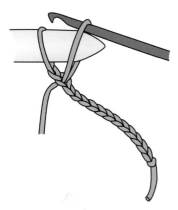

Part Two

Step 1: Insert the hook from left to right through first 5 loops on the needle. If the hook is inserted from right to left, the lace will angle in the opposite direction.

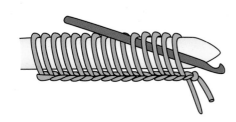

Step 2: Slip this group of 5 loops off the needle, twisting them from left to right, and work a sl st in the center of the group.

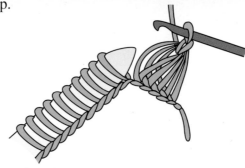

Step 3: Work 5 single crochet in center of group.

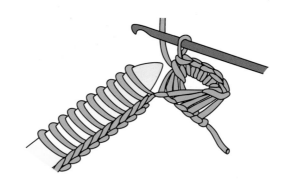

Step 4: Insert hook from left to right through next 5 loops on the needle.

Step 5: Slip this group of 5 loops off the needle, twisting them from left to right, and work 5 single crochet in the center of the group.

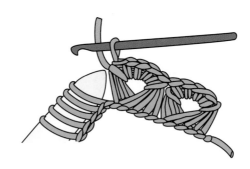

Step 6: Repeat steps 4 and 5 across the row. At the end of the row, there will be one loop on the crochet hook and no loops on the knitting needle.

To begin next row, repeat Step 1, inserting hook in each single crochet instead of each chain. Then repeat Steps 2 through 6.

Broomstick Lace Hat

Skill Level: Intermediate ■ ■ ■ □

Finished Size: Approx. 22" (55.88 cm) circumference

Materials:
Light worsted weight yarn ③ Light
[80% acrylic, 20% nylon, 3.5 ounces, 340 yards (100 grams, 310 meters)] per skein
  1 skein red
Note: *Photographed model made with Anne Geddes Baby™ Yarn #902 Ladybug.*
Size F/5 (3.75 mm) crochet hook or size required for
  gauge
1" diameter broomstick needle size 50 (25 mm)
Tapestry needle

Gauge: 4 groups of 4 lps = 4" (10.16 cm) wide; 2 rows of broomstick lace = 2¾" (7 cm)high

Instructions

Ch 88.

Row 1 (step 1): Holding broomstick needle in left hand with point facing right, slip lp from crochet hook onto needle, working from left to right across ch; *insert hook in next ch and draw up a lp, place lp onto needle; rep from * across: 88 lps on broomstick needle.

Row 1 (step 2): Insert hook from left to right through fir 4 lps on broomstick needle, slip these 4 lps off needle, being careful not to tighten first lp, ch 1, work 4 sc in center of same 4 lps (group made); *insert hook from lef to right through next 4 lps on needle, slip these 4 lps off needle and work 4 sc in center of same 4 lps; rep from * across; do NOT turn: 22 groups of 4 sc.

Row 2 (step 1): Working from left to right, working in back loop only; *draw up lp in next sc and place onto needle; rep from * across: 88 lps on broomstick needle.

Row 2 (step 2): Rep Row 1, step 2.

Rows 3 and 4: Rep Row 2, steps 1 and 2.

Row 5 (step 1): Rep Row 2, step 1.

Row 5 (step 2): Insert hook from left to right through fi 4 lps on broomstick needle, slip these 4 lps off needle, being careful not to tighten first lp, ch 1, work 2 sc in center of same 4 lps (group made); *insert hook from le to right through next 4 lps on needle, slip these 4 lps off needle and work 2 sc in center of same 4 lps; rep from * across; do NOT turn: 22 groups of 2 sc.

Row 6 (step 1): Rep Row 2, step 1: 44 lps on broomstic needle.

Row 6 (step 2): Insert hook from left to right through fi 4 lps on broomstick needle, slip these 4 lps off needle, being careful not to tighten first lp, ch 1, work 1 sc in center of same 4 lps (group made); *insert hook from le to right through next 4 lps on needle, slip these 4 lps of needle and work 1 sc in center of same 4 lps; rep from * across; do NOT turn: 11 sc. Finish off, leaving a long ta for sewing.

Assembly
Weave tail through 11 stitches on Row 6 and tighten. S back seam.

Bottom Edging
With right side facing, and hat upside down, working i free lps of each foundation ch, join with sl st in any ch, 1, sc in same ch as joining, sc in each rem ch around; j with sl st in first sc: 88 sc. Finish off.

Finishing
Weave in all ends.

Broomstick Lace Afghan

Designed by Janie Herrin

Skill Level: Intermediate ■■■□

Finished Size: Approx. 53" wide x 45" high (134.6 cm 114.3 cm), plus fringe

Materials:
Worsted weight yarn [4 Medium]
[100% acrylic, 7 ounces, 370 yards (198 grams, 338 meters)] per skein
1 skein each:
Light green (A)
Dark green (B)
Dark blue (C)
Light blue (D)
Light purple (E)
Dark purple (F)
Tan (G)
Off-white (H)

Note: *Photographed model made with Red Heart® With Love #1601 Lettuce, #1620 Clover, #1814 True Blue, #1502 Iced Aqua, #1538 Lilac, #1530 Violet, #1308 Tan and #1303 Aran.*

Size J/10 (6 mm) crochet hook (or size required for gauge)
1" diameter broomstick needle size 50 (25 mm)

Tapestry needle

Instructions continue on page 22

Gauge: 3 groups of 4 lps = 3¼" (8.3 cm) wide; 2 rows of broomstick lace = 2¾" (7 cm) high

Notes:
Leave long tails at beginning and end of rows to be added to fringe later.
If left-handed, work rows in opposite direction.
All rows are worked with right side facing.

Instructions

With A, ch 161.

Foundation Row (right side): Sc in back bar of 2nd ch from hook and in back bar of each rem ch across: 160 sc. Do NOT turn.

Row 1 (step 1): Holding broomstick needle in left hand with point facing right, slip lp from crochet hook onto needle, working from left to right across ch; *insert hook in next sc and draw up a lp, place lp onto needle; rep from * across: 160 lps on broomstick needle.

Row 1 (step 2): Insert hook from left to right through first 4 lps on broomstick needle, slip these 4 lps off needle, being careful not to tighten first lp, ch 1, work 4 sc in center of same 4 lps (group made); *insert hook from left to right through next 4 lps on needle, slip these 4 lps off needle and work 4 sc in center of same 4 lps; rep from * across; do NOT turn: 40 groups of 4 sc. Finish off.

Row 2 (step 1): With B, working from left to right, working in back loop only, draw up lp in first sc and place onto needle; *draw up lp in next sc and place onto needle; rep from * across: 160 lps on broomstick needle.

Row 2 (step 2): Rep Row 1, step 2.

Rows 3 through 8: Rep Row 2 (steps 1 and 2), 6 more times, changing color in each row and using next color color sequence (C-H) for each row (for example: Row in C, Row 4 in D, Row 5 in E, etc).

Rows 9 through 32: Rep Row 2 (steps 1 and 2), 24 mo times, changing color in each row and using next color color sequence (A-H) for each row.

Rows 33 through 38: Rep Row 2 (steps 1 and 2), 6 mo times, changing color in each row and using next color color sequence (A-F) for each row.

Fringe

Following Fringe instructions on page 64, cut strands o each color 12" long. Knot 3 strands of matching color a both ends of rows, including tails in fringe and making fringe at each end of each row. Trim fringe evenly.

ymbols for crochet instructions have been used for
ost 100 years in most countries in the world except in
English speaking world where our choice has been the
ted word. Today, however, it has become possible for
cheters to see crochet patterns from many countries.
patterns all are presented in symbol form, the
rnational visual language of crochet. This language is
nposed of symbols, each of which represents and looks
a crochet stitch. If you know this language, you can
k a design written for any audience, even if you can't
so much as "hello" in the language of the designer.

w To Do Symbol Crochet

Symbols

Symbol crochet each stitch is shown as a picture or
mbol that looks similar to the stitch itself. Shorter
ches are represented by shorter symbols while taller
ches are represented by taller symbols. These crochet
bols are sometimes grouped together, just as the
ches themselves can be grouped together.

ymbols can sometimes look slightly different from
publication to another. The slip stitch symbol can be
le as a dot or a black oval; the single crochet symbol
be made as an "x" or a "+". The short lines in the
dle of some of the other crochet symbols can be
ted or straight. In fact, all symbols may not be the
le size; they can be slanted, elongated or distorted to
better in a chart. Symbols are often grouped together,
as the stitches themselves are grouped together for
ches such as bobbles, clusters, shells or popcorns.

Diagrams

order to make the work easy to do, the symbols
laid out in a chart into rows or rounds just like
crochet project itself. These charts are called
Diagram." A diagram actually often looks like
finished piece, and will show how the piece is
structed.

e: Crochet charts are generally made for right-
ded crocheters. Left-handers may want to copy a
rt onto a transparency which can then be flipped over,
ing the pattern into the best direction for left-handers.

projects worked in rows, such as the scarf on page
the first row is located at the bottom of the chart, and
last row is at the top of the chart. Right side rows
read from right to left and wrong side rows are read

from left to right if you are right-handed and the opposite
if you are left-handed. Often charts worked in rows are
drawn with alternating colors of symbols for each row,
making it easier to follow each row in the chart.

In projects worked in rounds, such as the Doily on
page 24, begin in the center of the chart and work around
from right to left in a counterclockwise direction to the
outer edge of the chart, if you are right handed, and from
left to right (clockwise) if you are left-handed.

If you have never worked a project from a symbol
chart, or if you knew how but have forgotten, we are
giving you a chance to practice working a project from
symbols. First we give you the pattern in words. Then
on a following page, we give you the complete pattern.
Try working from the symbols, checking your work
with the words. A complete symbol crochet chart is
generally shown for small crochet projects. For large
crochet projects, it is common to only show a section
or "slice" of the project in the symbol chart because of
space limitations in the book or magazine. On page 26,
you will find an example of a symbol crochet pattern as
a "slice" for the doily. A slice chart will always show the
beginning of the project, a full repeat and the beginning/
end of the rows or rounds. The symbol chart will include
the row or round numbers, located near the beginning of
each row or round. Here are some of the most common
crochet symbols.

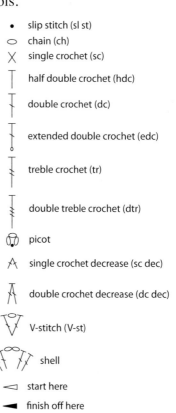

- slip stitch (sl st)
- chain (ch)
- single crochet (sc)
- half double crochet (hdc)
- double crochet (dc)
- extended double crochet (edc)
- treble crochet (tr)
- double treble crochet (dtr)
- picot
- single crochet decrease (sc dec)
- double crochet decrease (dc dec)
- V-stitch (V-st)
- shell
- start here
- finish off here

Symbol Crochet Doily

Skill Level: Intermediate ▬▬▬▭

Finished Size: Approx. 16½" (42 cm) diameter

Materials:
Size 10 crochet thread ⓪
[100% cotton, 350 yards (320 meters)] per ball
  1 ball rust
Note: *Photographed model made with Aunt Lydia's®
Classic Crochet Thread, size 10 #341 Russet.*
Size 7 (1.65 mm) steel crochet hook (or size required for
  gauge)
Tapestry needle

Gauge: Rnds 1 through 6 = 3¾" (9.53 cm) diameter

Stitch Guide

Shell: Work (2 dc, ch 2, 2 dc) in specified st or sp: shel
made.

Beginning shell (beg shell): (Sl st, ch 3, dc, ch 2, 2 dc
specified st or sp: beg shell made.

V-stitch (V-st): Work (dc, ch 1, dc) in specified st or sp
V-st made.

Double crochet decrease (dc dec): [YO, insert hook i
next st and draw up a lp, YO and draw through 2 lps on

ok] twice, YO and draw through all 3 lps on hook: dc
 made.

ot: Ch 3, sl st in 3rd ch from hook or in specified st:
ot made.

structions

d 1 (right side): Ch 6, join to form a ring; ch 3 (counts
dc here and throughout), 11 dc in ring; join with sl st in
ch of beg ch-3: 12 dc.

d 2: Ch 3, dc in same ch as joining, 2 dc in each rem dc
und; join as before: 24 dc.

d 3: Ch 7 (counts as dc and ch-4 sp); *skip next dc, dc
next dc, ch 4; rep from * around; join with sl st in 3rd ch
beg ch-7: 12 dc and 12 ch-4 sps.

d 4: Work beg shell in next ch-4 sp; *ch 2, V-st in next
4 sp, ch 2**, shell in next ch-4 sp; rep from * around,
ding last rep at **; join with sl st in 3rd ch of beg ch-3: 6
ells and 6 V-sts.

d 5: Sl st in next dc, work beg shell in ch-2 sp of first
ell; *ch 3, sc in next ch-2 sp, ch 3, V-st in ch-1 sp of next
st, ch 3, sc in next ch-2 sp, ch 3**, shell in ch-2 sp of
xt shell; rep from * around, ending last rep at **; join as
fore: 6 shells, 6 V-sts and 24 ch-3 sps.

d 6: Sl st in next dc, work beg shell in ch-2 sp of first
ell; *ch 5, sk next 2 ch-3 sps, V-st in ch-1 sp of next
st, ch 5, sk next 2 ch-3 sps**, shell in ch-2 sp of next
ell; rep from * around, ending last rep at **; join: 6
ells, 6 V-sts and 12 ch-5 sps.

d 7: Ch 3, dc in next dc; *2 dc in ch-2 sp of shell, dc in
xt 2 dc, 5 dc in next ch-5 sp, dc in next dc, dc in ch-1 sp
V-st, dc in next dc, 5 dc in next ch-5 sp**, dc in next 2
; rep from * around, ending last rep at **; join: 114 dc.

d 8: Ch 3, dc in same dc as joining; *dc in next 18
**, 2 dc in next dc; rep from * around, ending last rep at
; join: 120 dc.

d 9: Ch 8 (counts as dc and ch-5 sp); *skip next 3 dc,
 in next dc, ch 5; rep from * around, sk last 3 dc; join
th sl st in 3rd ch of beg ch-8: 30 dc and 30 ch-5 sps.

Rnd 10: Work beg shell in first ch-5 sp; *ch 3, V-st in next
ch-5 sp, ch 3**, shell in next ch-5 sp; rep from * around,
ending last rep at **; join: 15 shells and 15 V-sts.

Rnds 11 and 12: Sl st in next dc, work beg shell in ch-2
sp of first shell; *ch 3, V-st in ch-1 sp of next V-st, ch 3**,
shell in ch-2 sp of next shell; rep from * around, ending
last rep at **; join.

Rnd 13: Rep Rnd 5: 15 shells, 15 V-sts and 60 ch-3 sps.

Rnd 14: Rep Rnd 6: 15 shells, 15 V-sts and 30 ch-5 sps.

Rnd 15: Ch 3, dc in next dc; *2 dc in ch-2 sp of shell, dc
in next 2 dc, 4 dc in next ch-5 sp, dc in next dc, dc in ch-1
sp of V-st, dc in next dc, 4 dc in next ch-5 sp**, dc in next
2 dc; rep from * around, ending last rep at **; join: 255 dc.

Rnd 16: Ch 3, dc in next 82 dc, dc dec in next 2 dc, [dc in
next 83 dc, dc dec in next 2 dc] twice; join: 252 dc.

Rnd 17: Ch 3, dc in next dc and in each rem dc around;
join.

Rnd 18: Ch 3, dc in next 6 dc; *ch 5, skip next 2 dc, sc in
next 7 dc, ch 5, skip next 2 dc**; dc in next 7 dc; rep from
* around, ending last rep at **; join: 14 groups of 7 dc, 14
groups of 7 sc and 28 ch-5 sps.

Rnd 19: Ch 4 (counts as dc and ch-1 sp), dc in next dc, [ch
1, dc in next dc] 5 times; *ch 5, skip next sc, sc in next 6
sc, ch 5**, dc in next dc, [ch 1, dc in next dc] 6 times; rep
from * around, ending last rep at **; join with sl st in 3rd
ch of beg ch-4: 14 groups of 7 dc with ch-1 between each
dc, 14 groups of 6 sc and 28 ch-5 sps.

Rnd 20: Ch 4, dc in next dc, [ch 1, dc in next dc] 5 times;
*ch 5, sk next sc, sc in next 5 sc, ch 5**, dc in next dc, [ch
1, dc in next dc] 6 times; rep from * around, ending last
rep at **; join with sl st in 3rd ch of beg ch-4: 14 groups of
7 dc with ch-1 between each dc, 14 groups of 5 sc and 28
ch-5 sps.

Rnd 21: Ch 5 (counts as dc and ch-2 sp), dc in next dc, [ch
2, dc in next dc] 5 times; *ch 5, skip next sc, sc in next 4
sc, ch 5**, dc in next dc, [ch 2, dc in next dc] 6 times; rep
from * around, ending last rep at **; join with sl st in 3rd
ch of beg ch-5: 14 groups of 7 dc with ch-2 between each
dc, 14 groups of 4 sc and 28 ch-5 sps.

Instructions continued on page 26

Rnd 22: Ch 5 (counts as dc and ch-2 sp), dc in next dc, [ch 2, dc in next dc] 5 times; *ch 5, skip next sc, sc in next 3 sc, ch 5**, dc in next dc, [ch 2, dc in next dc] 6 times; rep from * around, ending last rep at **; join with sl st in 3rd ch of beg ch-5: 14 groups of 7 dc with ch-2 between each dc, 14 groups of 3 sc and 28 ch-5 sps.

Rnd 23: Ch 6 (counts as dc and ch-3 sp), dc in next dc, [ch 3, dc in next dc] 5 times; *ch 5, skip next sc, sc in next 2 sc, ch 5**, dc in next dc, [ch 3, dc in next dc] 6 times; rep from * around, ending last rep at **; join with sl st in 3rd ch of beg ch-6: 14 groups of 7 dc with ch-3 between each dc, 14 groups of 2 sc and 28 ch-5 sps.

Rnd 24: Ch 7 (counts as dc and ch-4 sp), dc in next dc, [ch 4, dc in next dc] 5 times; *ch 5, skip next sc, sc in next sc, ch 5**, dc in next dc, [ch 4, dc in next dc] 6 times; rep from * around, ending last rep at **; join with

sl st in 3rd ch of beg ch-7: 14 groups of 7 dc with ch-4 between each dc, 14 sc and 28 ch-5 sps.

Rnd 25: Ch 8 (counts as dc and ch-5 sp), dc in next dc, [ch 5, dc in next dc] 5 times; *ch 2, skip next sc**, dc in next dc, [ch 5, dc in next dc] 6 times; rep from * around, ending last rep at **; join with sl st in 3rd ch of beg ch-8: 14 groups of 7 dc with ch-5 between each dc and 14 ch-2 sps.

Rnd 26: Sl st in next 2 chs, ch 1, sc in next ch; *[ch 3, picot, ch 3, sc in next ch-5 sp] 5 times, ch 3, dc in next ch-2 sp, picot in top of last dc made, ch 3**, sc in next ch-5 sp; rep from * around, ending last rep at **; join with sl st in first sc: 84 picots. Finish off; weave in ends.

Wash and block.

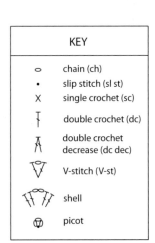

KEY	
o	chain (ch)
•	slip stitch (sl st)
X	single crochet (sc)
⊤	double crochet (dc)
⋀	double crochet decrease (dc dec)
⋁	V-stitch (V-st)
⫟⫟	shell
⊕	picot

...ill Level: Intermediate ■■■□

...nished Size: Approx. 6½" wide x 60" long (16.5 cm ... 52.4 cm) plus fringe

...aterials:

...e 3 crochet thread
...0% cotton, 150 yards/137 meters] per ball
... balls green
...te: *Photographed model made with Aunt Lydia's®*
...*ochet Thread Fashion 3™, size 3 #625 Sage.*
...e F/5 (3.75 mm) crochet hook (or size required for ...auge)
...pestry needle

Gauge: 20 sc = 4" (10.16 cm)
12 rows in pattern (8 sc rows and 4 V-st rows) = 3" (7.62 cm)

Stitch Guide

V-stitch (V-st): Work (dc, ch 2, dc) in specified st or sp: V-st made.

Single crochet decrease (sc dec): [Insert hook in next st and draw up a lp] twice, YO and draw through all 3 lps on hook: sc dec made.

Instructions

Row 1 (right side): Ch 33, sc in 2nd ch from hook and in each rem ch across: 32 sc; ch 1, turn.

Instructions continued on page 28

27

Rows 2 and 3: Sc in each sc across; ch 1, turn.

Row 4: Sc in each sc across; ch 4 (counts as dc and ch-1 sp on following row here and throughout), turn.

Row 5: Skip first sc, skip next sc, V-st in next sc; *ch 1, skip next 2 sc, V-st in next sc; rep from * across to last 2 sc; ch 1, skip next sc, dc in last sc: 10 V-sts and 2 dc; ch 4, turn.

Row 6: Skip first ch-1 sp, V-st in ch-2 sp of next V-st; *ch 1, sk next ch-1 sp, V-st in ch-2 sp of next V-st; rep from * across to beg ch-4; ch 1, dc in 3rd ch of beg ch-4; ch 1, turn.

Row 7: Sc in first dc; *sc in next ch-1 sp, 2 sc in ch-2 sp of next V-st; rep from * across to beg ch-4; sc in ch-4 sp, sc in 3rd ch of beg ch-4: 33 sc; ch 1, turn.

Row 8: Sc in first 15 sc, sc dec in next 2 sc, sc in last 16 sc: 32 sc; ch 1, turn.

Row 9: Sc in each sc across; ch 1, turn.

Row 10: Sc in each sc across; ch 4, turn.

Rep Rows 5 through 10 until scarf measures approx. 60 long. At end of last row, do not ch 4. Finish off; weave i ends.

Fringe
Following Fringe instructions on page 64, cut strands of each color 10" (25.4 cm) long. Knot 3 strands in each fringe, making 1 fringe in every other st across each sh edge. Trim fringe evenly.

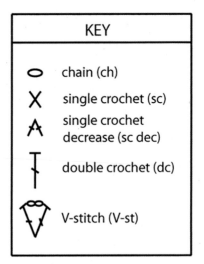

KEY	
O	chain (ch)
X	single crochet (sc)
A	single crochet decrease (sc dec)
T	double crochet (dc)
V	V-stitch (V-st)

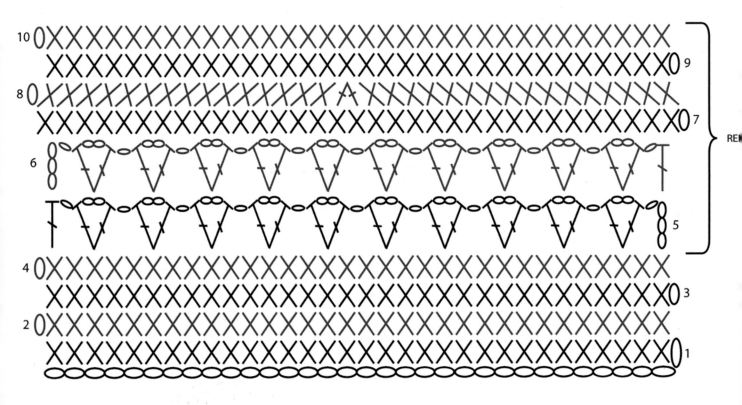

n the nineteenth century, women's hair styles required
use of large numbers of hairpins. To add a bit of
mour, these pins were often made in ivory or gold
d silver. During this period, literally miles and miles
lace was created and used to decorate clothes and
usehold linens. Eventually actual looms modeled on
original hairpin were made. In the beginning, the
ms, sometimes called forks, staples or frames, were
de in one width. So if the crocheter wanted to use
eral widths of lace, she needed to have a collection
looms. Today most hairpin lace looms are adjustable
dth. Whatever type of loom you use, basically, hairpin
e is made in vertical strips formed by wrapping the
n around the loom, while creating a center spine with
chet stitches. Although there are many ways to create
strip, sometimes called a braid, most patterns call for
basic strip. Projects may differ in the methods that are
d to join the strips.

ow To Do Hairpin Lace

p 1: Set up the loom by adjusting it to the width called
in the pattern.

p 2: Make a loose slipknot and place it over the left-
d loom bar, centering the knot between the two bars.
ap the yarn around the right bar from front to back;
ert the hook through the left slip knot loop and hook
wrapped yarn.

p 3: Draw the hooked yarn through the slip knot loop
then chain 1.

Step 4: Keep the yarn behind the left bar and flip the loom
to the left. Be sure to rotate the hook so that the handle
faces up before the loom is flipped.

Step 5: Insert the hook under the front strand of the left
loop and draw up a loop, yarn over and complete the
single crochet. This single crochet starts the center spine
that holds the loops together.

Repeat Steps 4 and 5 for the desired strip length. Keep the
center spine straight and centered between the two bars as
you work; you may find it easier to remove the hook from
the work as you flip the loom.

The above instructions are for working with single
crochet. The lace may also be worked with two single
crochet stitches or with double crochet:

Joining the Strips
No matter which method is used to create the strip, the
strips must be joined.

Joining with Crochet Hook
Place the two strips together horizontally. Using the
crochet hook, lift one of the loops from the first strip
and one from the second. Draw the second loop through
the first. Then pick up the second loop of the first strip.
Draw this through the loop on the hook. Then pick up
the second loop from the second strip and draw the loop
through. Continue in this way along the strips until they
are joined together. Make certain that the final stitch is
securely sewn to prevent it unraveling.

Joining with Chain Stitch
Place two strips together horizontally and work from right
to left. Make a slip knot and place on crochet hook. *Insert
the hook though first loop of first strip and first loop of
second strip, yarn over the hook and draw through all
loops. Repeat from * in the next loop of each strip until
all the loops are joined. Finish off thread by drawing it
through the last stitch.

Hairpin Lace Stole

nished Size: Approx. 27" wide x 72" long (68.6 cm
82.9 cm)

aterials:
ngering weight yarn 🔒 Lace
% super kid mohair, 30% silk, 0.88 ounces, 231 yards
grams, 212 meters)] per ball]
balls black

te: *Photographed model made with Lion Brand® LB
llection® Silk Mohair #153 Midnight.*

e G/6 (4 mm) crochet hook (or size required for gauge)
rpin lace loom, 2" (5cm) wide

auge:
rpin lace strip with 29 loops on each side and 2 rnds of
ing worked = 4½" wide x 8" long (11.4 cm x 20.3 cm)

tch Guide

uble crochet decrease (dc dec): [YO, insert hook in
t st and draw up a lp, YO and draw through 2 lps on
ok] twice, YO and draw through all 3 lps on hook: dc
made.

structions

irpin Lace Strips (make 6)
ke a strip of hairpin lace with 263 loops on each side
oom. Finish off.

ging Strips and Joining Strips

st Strip
d 1 (right side): Join with sc in first 11 lps, inserting
ok through all 11 lps at once (cluster made); *[ch 3, sc
next lp] 7 times; ch 3, sc through next 11 lps at once
uster made); rep from * 13 more times; ch 3, sc in
ter sc of hairpin lace strip; working across opposite
e of strip, [ch 3, sc in next lp] 9 times, ch 3,
hrough next 11 lps at once (cluster made);
ch 3, sc in next lp] 7 times, ch 3, sc through next 11
 at once (cluster made); rep from * 12 more times;
3, sc in next lp] 9 times, ch 3, sc in center of hairpin
e strip, ch 3: 29 clusters and 236 ch-3 sps.

d 2: Work 5 sc in each of next 8 ch-3 sps; *5 sc in next
3 sp (after cluster), 2 sc in next ch-3 sp, ch 5, turn; sk
t 14 sc, sl st in next sc, ch 1, turn; 7 sc in ch-5 sp just
de (scallop made), 3 sc in same ch-3 sp on Rnd 1 as
 (before ch-5), 2 sc in next ch-3 sp, ch 5, turn; sl st

in center sc of scallop, ch 5, sk next 4 sc worked in ch-3
sps, sl st in center sc of 5 sc worked in next ch-3 sp, ch 1,
turn; 7 sc in each of next 2 ch-5 sps (2 scallops made and
triangle with 3 scallops completed), 3 sc in same ch-3 sp
on Rnd 1 as 2 sc (before ch-5)***, 5 sc in each of next 5
ch-3 sps**; rep from * to ** 12 more times; rep from * to
*** once; working across opposite side, 5 sc in each of next
8 ch-3 sps; rep from * to ** 13 more times; rep from * to
*** once; 5 sc in each of next 8 ch-3 sps, sl st in next 8 sc,
ch 5, turn; sk next 15 sc, sl st in next sc, ch 1, turn; 7 sc in
ch-5 sp just made (scallop made), sl st in next 5 sc, ch 5,
turn; sl st in center sc of scallop, ch 5, sl st in center sc of 5
sc worked in next ch-3 sp, ch 1, turn; 7 sc in each of next
2 ch-5 sps (2 scallops made and triangle with 3 scallops
completed); join with sl st in next sc: 15 triangles on first
side and 14 triangles on 2nd side. Finish off; weave in ends.

Note: *Strips are joined together while working Rnd 2
of Edging. Each side with 15 triangles is joined to 15
triangle side of adjacent strip. Each side with 14 triangles
is joined to 14 triangle side of adjacent strip.*

2nd Strip
Rnd 1: Work same as Rnd 1 of First Strip.

Rnd 2: Work 5 sc in each of next 4 ch-3 sps, joining to 15
triangle side of First Strip, sk first triangle of First Strip,
join with sl st in corresponding st on First Strip, 5 sc in
each of next 4 ch-3 sps on 2nd Strip; *5 sc in next ch-3 sp
(after cluster), 2 sc in next ch-3 sp, ch 5, turn; sk first 14 sc,
sl st in next sc, ch 1, turn; 7 sc in ch-5 sp just made (scallop
made), 3 sc in same ch-3 sp on Rnd 1 as 2 sc (before ch-5),
2 sc in next ch-3 sp, ch 5, turn; sl st in center sc of scallop,
ch 5, sk next 4 sc worked in ch-3 sps, sl st in center sc of
5 sc worked in next ch-3 sp, ch 1, turn; 4 sc in next ch-5
sp (scallop started), join with sl st in corresponding st of
opposite triangle on First Strip, 3 sc in same ch-5 sp on
2nd Strip (scallop completed), 4 sc in next ch-5 sp (scallop
started), join with sl st in corresponding st of same triangle
on First Strip, 3 sc in same ch-5 sp on 2nd Strip (scallop and
triangle with 3 scallops completed), 3 sc in same ch-3 sp on
Rnd 1 as 2 sc (before ch-5)***, 5 sc in next ch-3 sp, join in
corresponding st on First Strip, 5 sc in each of next 4 ch-3
sps**; rep from * to ** 12 more times; rep from * to ***
once; working across opposite side, 5 sc in each of next 8
ch-3 sps; rep from * to ** on Rnd 2 of First Strip 13 more
times; rep from * to *** on Rnd 2 of First Strip once; 5 sc
in each of next 8 ch-3 sps, sl st in next 8 sc, ch 5, turn; sk
next 15 sc, sl st in next sc, ch 1, turn; 7 sc in ch-5 sp just
made (scallop made), sl st in next 5 sc, ch 5, turn; sl st in
center sc of scallop, ch 5, sl st in center sc of 5 sc worked

Instructions continued on page 32 31

in next ch-3 sp, ch 1, turn; 4 sc in next ch-5 sp (scallop started), join in corresponding st of skipped triangle on First Strip, 3 sc in same ch-5 sp of 2nd Strip (scallop completed), 4 sc in next ch-5 sp (scallop started), join in corresponding st of same triangle on First Strip, 3 sc in same ch-5 sp on 2nd Strip (scallop and triangle with 3 scallops completed); join with sl st in next sc: 15 joined triangles on first side and 14 triangles on 2nd side. Finish off; weave in ends.

3rd Strip
Rnd 1: Work same as Rnd 1 of First Strip.

Rnd 2: Work 5 sc in each of next 8 ch-3 sps; *5 sc in next ch-3 sp (after cluster), 2 sc in next ch-3 sp, ch 5, turn; sk first 14 sc, sl st in next sc, ch 1, turn; 7 sc in ch-5 sp just made (scallop made), 3 sc in same ch-3 sp on Rnd 1 as 2 sc (before ch-5), 2 sc in next ch-3 sp, ch 5, turn; sl st in center sc of scallop, ch 5, sk next 4 sc worked in ch-3 sps, sl st in center sc of 5 sc worked in next ch-3 sp, ch 1, turn; 7 sc in each of next 2 ch-5 sps (2 scallops made and triangle with 3 scallops completed), 3 sc in same ch-3 sp on Rnd 1 as 2 sc (before ch-5)***, 5 sc in each of next 5 ch-3 sps**; rep from * to ** 12 more times; rep from * to *** once; working across opposite side, 5 sc in each of next 4 ch-3 sps, joining to 14 triangle side of 2nd Strip, join with sl st in

corresponding st of 2nd Strip, [5 sc in each of next 5 ch-3 sps, 2 sc in next ch-3 sp, ch 5, turn; sk first 14 sc, sl st in next sc, ch 1, turn; 7 sc in ch-5 sp just made (scallop made), 3 sc in same ch-3 sp on Rnd 1 as 2 sc (before ch-5), 2 sc in next ch-3 sp, ch 5, turn; sl st in center sc of scallop, ch 5, sk next 4 sc worked in ch-3 sps, sl st in center sc of 5 sc worked in next ch-3 sp, ch 1, turn; 4 sc in next ch-5 sp (scallop started), join with sl st in corresponding st of opposite triangle of 2nd Strip, 3 sc in same ch-5 sp on 3rd Strip, 4 sc in next ch-5 sp, join to corresponding st of same triangle of 2nd Strip, 3 sc in same ch-5 sp on 3rd Strip, 3 sc in same ch-3 sp on Rnd 1 as 2 sc (before ch-5), 5 sc in next ch-3 sp, join with sl st in corresponding st of 2nd Strip] 14 times; 5 sc in each of next 7 ch-3 sps, sl st in next 8 sc, ch 5, turn; sk next 15 sc, sl st in next sc, ch 1, turn; 7 sc in ch-5 sp just made (scallop made), sl st in next 5 sc, ch 5, turn; sl st in center sc of scallop, ch 5, sk next 4 sc worked in ch-3 sps, sl st in center sc of 5 sc worked in next ch-3 sp, ch 1, turn; 7 sc in each of next 2 ch-5 sps (2 scallops made and triangle with 3 scallops completed); join with sl st in next sc: 22 triangles on first side and 21 joined triangles on 2nd side. Finish off; weave in ends.

Join 4th Strip to 3rd Strip in same manner as 2nd Strip.
Join 5th Strip to 4th Strip in same manner as 3rd Strip.
Join 6th Strip to 5th Strip in same manner as 2nd Strip.

Stole Edging
With right side facing, join with sl st in 14th sc before first triangle of First Strip, working on long side, ch 3, dc in next sc, dc dec in next 2 sts; *dc in next 3 sc, dc dec in next 2 sts; rep from * across long side, ending in 18th st after last triangle; **ch 1, sk next sc, dc in next sc; rep from ** across short scalloped end, work other long side and short scalloped end in same manner; join with sl st in 3rd ch of beg ch-3. Finish off; weave in ends.

Wash and block to finished measurements.

Hairpin Lace Scarf

Skill Level: Intermediate ■■■□

Finished Size: Approx. 6" wide x 51" long, [1]5.2 cm x 129.5 cm) plus fringe

Materials:
[Wo]rsted weight yarn [4 Medium]
[10]0% acrylic, 3.5 ounces, 170 yards (100 grams, 156 [met]ers)] per skein
[1]skein red
1 skein orange
1 skein yellow
1 skein green

Note: *Photographed model made with Lion Brand® Vanna's Choice® #180 Cranberry, #134 Terra Cotta, #158 Mustard and #174 Olive.*

Size I/9 (5.5 mm) crochet hook or size required for gauge

Hairpin lace loom, 3" (7.5 cm) wide

6" (15.2 cm) piece of cardboard (for fringe)

Gauge:

Hairpin lace strip with 14 loops on each side = 4¼" long x 3" (10.8 cm x 7.6 cm) wide (before weaving strips together)

Instructions

Hairpin Lace Strips
(make 4 strips: 1 with each color)
Make a strip of hairpin lace with 166 loops on each side of loom. Finish off.

Joining Strips
Lay two strips side by side on a table. Put crochet hook through first 2 lps on first strip. Now put hook through first 2 lps on 2nd strip and pull them through the 2 lps already on hook. With these 2 lps still on hook, pick up the next 2 lps on first strip and pull them through. Continue in this manner, alternating first and 2nd strips, until all loops have been worked. Secure lps at top with tail of strip. Join 3rd to 2nd and 4th to 3rd strip in same manner. Secure lps at top. Finish outside edges by pulling 2 lps through 2 lps all the way to the top. Secure lps at top.

Fringe
Following Fringe instructions on page 64, cut strands of each color 12" long. Knot 4 strands of matching color in ends of strips, making 2 fringe at each end of each strip (8 fringe at each end of scarf). Trim fringe evenly.

IRISH CROCHET

Producing lace has long been a tradition in Ireland, dating back to the sixteenth century when it was called Nun's work, an appropriate name since it was developed in Irish convents as an imitation of Venetian Rose Point Lace.

What we now know of as Irish Crochet, however, did not really develop until the middle of the nineteenth century. At that time fashion called for the wearing of lace; even men wore lace evening shirts and jabots. The main income producer in the country at that time was the growing of potatoes, but a potato blight had almost completely destroyed the agricultural industry, and Ireland was in the midst of a terrible famine. There could be a huge market for producing lace if it could be manufactured with speed. Making beautiful lace was extremely time consuming, and the people needed something that could be produced quickly.

Today it is generally accepted that Mademoiselle Riego de la Blanchardiere actually invented the style we know today as Irish Crochet. Born in England to a Spanish father and an Irish mother, Mlle Riego reasoned that Spanish Needle Lace, which was very similar to the very desirable Venetian Rose Point lace could not only be made with a crochet hook but was at least 10 times faster. She eventually published the first book of Irish Crochet patterns in 1846. Schools teaching crochet began to spring up, and her book was used not only in the schools but also in the constantly growing cottage industry creating crochet lace.

Eventually entire families became involved in the making of lace as a way of surviving. Since all levels could do the work, everyone in the family, including men and children were involved. The difficult patterns might be the work of the most experienced crocheter, but the simple leaves and stems could be worked even by young children. Often one person made the same piece over and over.

Historians feel that Irish Crochet was one of the factors that succeeded in saving Ireland. The making of lace served as a vital cottage industry throughout the famine. In the years following the famine, the interest in Irish Crochet declined, and eventually the demand for lace declined. Today, however, Irish Crochet remains as one of the most beautiful of crochet techniques. Traditional Irish Crochet was made by first crocheting many small motifs, then crocheting a net-like background and working the mesh between the motifs. Because the crocheter did not work in rows or rounds, she (or he) was free to show off her individuality and design skill. It would have been very rare for two crocheters working the same motifs to turn out the same results.

The motifs—usually flowers, shamrocks, vines, sprays, leaves, etc.—were crocheted and then placed face down the desired position onto a piece of scrap fabric or paper and secured temporarily. This tracing, in addition to hav the outlines of the motifs, would have had auxiliary line which indicated the direction to be followed in the work of the mesh forming the background. Everything having been prepared, the mesh was worked. Finally the spaces between the stitches were filled with bars of crochet, and the paper or fabric removed.

A characteristic of the working of the motifs was that t first crochet stitches were worked over a round packing or "padding" cord instead of into a crochet chain, as in ordinary crochet. While it is possible to follow the patter without the use of padding cord, to achieve the look of traditional Irish crochet, a padding cord should be used.

How To Do Irish Crochet

Step 1: Make the required number of chains and join with a slip stitch.

Step 1

Step 2: Cut a piece of thread about three or four times longer than the chain made in step 1. Wrap the thread around the chain, and hold it in place.

Step 2

Step 3: Work the required stitches over the chain and the padding threads. When the motif has been completed, pull the ends of the padding thread through several stitches.

Step 3

The technique for creating Irish Crochet is really a simple one. The rules were few. It has been the same fo over 100 years. Here is what was published in 1909 in famous Priscilla Irish Crochet Book. The rules still ap *"There are two threads, as it were, used in working thi lace. One is the working thread, which is used to make the stitches; the other thread, or cord is only used to w over, which gives this lace the rich effect so different from ordinary crochet work. This cord is sometimes he close to the work and the stitches are made over it into the row of stitches made before (working only in the ba loops) or the stitches are worked over it alone, using it as a foundation. In making Irish crochet the stitches should be uniform, close and compact; loose or ragge crochet makes inferior lace, wanting in crispness, and padding cord should never show through the work."*

ish Crochet Edgings

Note: *To join with sc, make a slip knot and place on hook, insert hook in specified st and draw up a lp, YO and draw through both lps on hook.*

se Edging

ill Level: Intermediate ▭▭▭▭▭

nished Size: Approx. 4½" (11.4 cm) wide x desired gth

aterials:
e 10 crochet Thread 🔘 Lace
0% cotton, 400 yards (365 meters)] per ball
ball white

te: *Photographed model made with Aunt Lydia's® ssic Crochet Thread, size 10 #1 White.*
e 7 (1.65 mm) steel crochet hook (or size required or gauge)
estry needle

auge: Rnds 1 through 4 of rose motif = 1⅝" (4 cm) meter

tch Guide

uble crochet decrease (dc dec): *Yo, insert hook in t specified st and draw up a lp, YO and draw through s on hook; rep from * in 2ⁿᵈ specified st, YO and draw ough all 3 lps on hook: dc dec made.

ginning cluster (beg CL): Ch 2, [YO, insert hook in cified st or sp and draw up a lp, YO and draw through s on hook] twice, YO and draw through all 3 lps on k: beg CL made.

ster (CL): [YO, insert hook in specified st or sp and w up a lp, YO and draw through 2 lps on hook] 3 times, and draw through all 4 lps on hook: CL made.

ot: Ch 4, sl st in top of last sc made before ch-4: picot de.

Instructions

First Rose Motif

Rnd 1 (right side): Ch 5, join with sl st to form a ring; ch 6 (counts as dc and ch-3 sp), [dc in ring, ch 3] 5 times; join with sl st in 3ʳᵈ ch of beg ch-6: 6 dc and 6 ch-3 sps.

Rnd 2: In each ch-3 sp work (sc, hdc, 3 dc, hdc, sc) for petal: 6 petals.

Rnd 3: *Working behind petals of Rnd 2, sc in next dc of Rnd 1 between petals, ch 5; rep from * around; join with sl st in first sc: 6 ch-5 sps.

Rnd 4: In each ch-5 sp work (sc, hdc, 5 dc, hdc, sc) for petal: 6 petals.

Rnd 5: *Working behind petals of Rnd 4, sc in next sc of Rnd 3 between petals, ch 7; rep from * around; join with sl st in first sc: 6 ch-7 sps.

Rnd 6: In each ch-7 sp work (sc, dc, 7 tr, dc, sc) for petal; join with sl st in first sc: 6 petals. Finish off; weave in ends.

Rose Edging

Rnd 1: With right side facing, join with sc in center tr of any petal; *ch 7, work dc dec, working first leg of st in last tr of same petal and 2ⁿᵈ leg of st in first tr of next petal, ch 7**, sc in center tr of same petal; rep from * around, ending last rep at **; join with sl st in first sc: 12 ch-7 sps.

Rnd 2: Sl st in first 2 chs of first ch-7 sp, work (beg CL, ch 9, CL) in same ch-7 sp (corner made); *[ch 7, (sc, ch 3, sc) in next ch-7 sp] twice, ch 7**, (CL, ch 9, CL) in next ch-7 sp (corner made); rep from * around, ending last rep at **; join with sl st in top of beg CL: 8 CL, 4 corner ch-9 sps, 12 ch-7 sps and 8 ch-3 sps. Finish off; weave in ends.

Second Rose
Make Rose Motif same as First Rose Motif.

Rose Edging

Rnd 1: Work same as Rnd 1 of Rose Edging on First Rose Motif.

Instructions continued on page 36

Rnd 2: Sl st in first 2 chs of first ch-7 sp, work beg CL in same ch-7 sp, ch 4, join with sl st in corner ch-9 sp of previous rose, ch 4, CL in same ch-7 sp on current rose, [ch 3, sc in next ch-7 sp on previous rose, ch 3, (sc, ch 3, sc) in next ch-7 sp on current rose] twice, ch 3, sc in next ch-7 sp on previous rose, ch 3, CL in next ch-7 sp on current rose, ch 4, join with sl st in corner ch-9 sp of previous rose, ch 4, CL in same ch-7 sp on current rose; *[ch 7, (sc, ch 3, sc) in next ch-7 sp] twice, ch 7**, (CL, ch 9, CL) in next ch-7 sp; rep from * around, ending last rep at **; join with sl st in top of beg CL: 8 CL, 4 ch-9 sps (2 joined to previous motif), 12 ch-7 sps (3 joined to previous motif) and 8 ch-3 sps. Finish off; weave in ends.

Work as many Rose Motifs as desired. Join each motif to previous motif while working Rose Edging in same manner as Second Rose Edging.

Top Edging

Row 1: With right side facing, join with sl st in 5th ch of corner ch-9 sp of first Rose Edging (in corner before joined Rose Motifs), ch 8 (counts as dc and ch-5 sp); *2 sc in next ch-7 sp, [ch 7, 2 sc in next ch-7 sp] twice, ch 5**, dc in motif joining, ch 5; rep from * across, ending last rep at **; dc in 5th ch of corner ch-9 sp on last Rose Edging: 2 ch-7 sps and 2 ch-5 sps across edge of each Rose Edging. Finish off; weave in ends.

Row 2: With right side facing, join with sc in 3rd ch of beg ch-8; *4 sc in next ch-5 sp, sc in next sc, picot, sc in next sc, [6 sc in next ch-7 sp, sc in next sc, picot, sc in next sc] twice, 4 sc in next ch-5 sp, sc in next dc**, picot; rep from * across, ending last rep at **: 3 picots between corners of each Rose Edging and 1 picot between roses. Finish off; weave in ends.

Bottom Edging

Row 1: With right side facing, join with sc in 5th ch of corner ch-9 sp on first Rose Edging (in corner before joined Rose Motifs); *[ch 8, sc in next ch-7 sp] 3 times, ch 8**, sc in motif joining, rep from * across, ending last rep at **; sc in 5th ch of corner ch-9 sp on last Rose Edging; ch 6 (counts as tr and ch-2 sp on following row), turn: 4 ch-8 sps across edge of each Rose Edging.

Row 2: Sc in next ch-8 sp; *[ch 8, sc in next ch-8 sp] 3 times**, ch 4, sc in next ch-8 sp; rep from * across, ending last rep at **; ch 2, tr in first sc; ch 1, turn: 3 ch-8 sps across edge of each Rose Edging with 1 ch-4 sp between Rose Edgings and 1 ch-2 sp at each end of edging.

Row 3: Sc in tr, 3 sc in next ch-2 sp; *[(5 sc, picot, 5 sc in next ch-8 sp] 3 times**, 5 sc in next ch-4 sp; rep from * across, ending last rep at **; 3 sc in last ch-6 sp, sc in 4th ch of same ch-6 sp: 3 picots across edge of each Rose Edging. Finish off; weave in ends.

Finishing
Wash and block.

Leaf Edging

Skill Level: Intermediate

Finished Size: Approx 2³⁄₄" (7 cm) wide x desired length

Materials:
Cotton crochet thread, size 10
[100% cotton, 400 yards (365 meters)] per ball
  1 ball white
Note: *Photographed model made with Aunt Lydia's ® Classic Crochet Thread, size 10 in #1 White.*
Size 7 (1.65 mm) steel crochet hook (or size required for gauge)
Tapestry needle

Gauge: Leaf = 1½" wide x 2³⁄₈" high (3.81 cm x 6 cm

Stitch Guide
Double treble crochet decrease (dtr dec): *YO 3 times, insert hook in first specified st and draw up a lp, [YO and draw through 2 lps on hook] 3 times; rep from * in 2nd specified st, YO and draw through all 3 lps on hook: dtr dec made.

Double treble crochet (dtr): YO 3 times, insert hook in specified st or sp and draw up a lp (5 lps on hook), [YO and draw through 2 lps on hook] 4 times: dtr made.

te: *To join with sc, make a slip knot and place on hook, ...ert hook in specified st and draw up a lp, YO and draw ...ugh both lps on hook.*

...structions

...st Leaf

...rting at center of leaf, ch 16.

...d 1 (right side): Sc in 2nd ch from hook and in each ch ...oss to last ch, 3 sc in last ch; working along opposite ...e of foundation chain, sc in next 13 chs, 2 sc in last ch ...same ch as first sc): 32 sc.

...te: *Working in back lp only, work now proceeds in* ...s.

...w 1: Sc in next 13 sc; ch 1, turn: 13 sc.

...w 2: Sc in first 13 sc, 3 sc in next sc, sc in next 13 sc; ...1, turn: 29 sc.

...w 3: Sc in first 14 sc, 3 sc in next sc, sc in next 11 sc; ...1, turn, leaving last 3 sc unworked: 28 sc.

...w 4: Sc in first 12 sc, 3 sc in next sc, sc in next 12 sc; ...1, turn, leaving last 3 sc unworked: 27 sc.

...w 5: Sc in first 13 sc, 3 sc in next sc, sc in next 10 sc; ...1, turn, leaving last 3 sc unworked: 26 sc.

...w 6: Sc in first 11 sc, 3 sc in next sc, sc in next 11 sc; ...1, turn, leaving last 3 sc unworked: 25 sc.

...w 7: Sc in first 12 sc; join with sl st in next sc: 12 sc. ...ish off; weave in ends.

...cond Leaf

...rk same as Rnd 1 and Rows 1 through 6 on First Leaf.

...w 7: Sl st in corresponding sc on First Leaf (in first sc ...Row 6), sc in first 12 sc on current leaf; join with sl st ...next sc: 12 sc. Finish off; weave in ends.

...ditional Leaves

...rk same as Second Leaf, joining each leaf to previous ...f, for desired length of edging.

Edging

Row 1: With right side facing, join with sl st in 6th sc before center sc on first leaf, ch 10 (counts as dtr and ch-5 sp); *ch 5, work dtr dec, working first leg of st in 6th sc from center sc on same leaf and 2nd leg of st in 6th sc from center sc on next leaf, ch 5, sc in center sc on same leaf; rep from * across; ch 5, dtr in 6th sc after center sc on same leaf; ch 4 (counts as dc and ch-1 sp on following row), turn.

Row 2: Sk first sc, sk next ch, dc in next ch; *ch 1, sk next ch, dc in next st (in ch, dtr dec or sc); rep from * across, working last dc in 5th ch of beg ch-10. Finish off; weave in ends.

Finishing

Wash and block. If desired, weave ribbon through spaces on Row 2 of edging; secure ends.

Shamrock Edging

Skill Level: Intermediate ◼◼◼◻

Finished Size: Approx 3" (7.62 cm) wide x desired length

Materials:

Size 10 crochet thread
[100% cotton, 400 yards (365 meters)] per ball
   1 ball white
Note: *Photographed model made with Aunt Lydia's® Classic Crochet Thread, size 10   #1 White.*
Size 7 (1.65 mm) steel crochet hook (or size required for gauge)
Tapestry needle

Instructions continued on page 38

Gauge: Rnds 1 and 2 of shamrock = $1\frac{3}{4}$" (4.45 cm) wide x $2\frac{1}{4}$" (5.71 cm) high

Stitch Guide

Picot: Ch 4, sc in 4th ch from hook: picot made.

Treble crochet decrease (tr dec): *Yo twice, insert hook in first specified st and draw up a lp, [YO and draw through 2 lps on hook] twice; rep from * in 2nd specified st, YO and draw through all 3 lps on hook: tr dec made.

Instructions

First Shamrock

Cut 2 pieces of thread, 20" long for padding cord. Fold in half and set aside.

Ch 29.

Rnd 1 (right side): Sl st in 14th ch from hook, [ch 13, sl st in same ch] twice: 3 ch-lps for petals and 15 chs for stem.

Rnd 2: Working over padding cord throughout this rnd, work 25 sc in each ch-lp, work 15 sc over remainder of foundation ch for stem, working last sc in last ch: 3 petals with 25 sc each and 1 stem with 15 sc (90 sc total).

Rnd 3: Sc in same ch as last sc worked, [*ch 3, picot, ch 3, sk first 9 sc on next petal, sc in next sc, ch 3, picot, ch 3, sk next 5 sc on same petal, sc in next sc, ch 3, picot, ch 3**, tr between this petal and next petal] twice; rep from * to ** once; sk first 7 sc on stem, sc in next sc, ch 3, picot, ch 3; join with sl st in first sc: 10 picots. Finish off; weave in ends.

Second Shamrock

Cut 2 pieces of size 10 thread, 20" long for padding cord. Fold in half and set aside.

Rnds 1 and 2: Work same as Rnds 1 and 2 on First Shamrock.

Rnd 3: Sc in same ch as last sc worked, [*ch 3, picot, ch 3, sk first 9 sc on next petal, sc in next sc**, ch 3, picot, ch 3, sk next 5 sc on same petal, sc in next sc, ch 3, picot, ch 3, tr between this petal and next petal] twice; rep from * to ** once; ch 5, sl st in corresponding picot on previous shamrock (in 2nd picot made on previous shamrock), ch 2,

sc in 4th ch worked of ch-5 (joined picot made), ch 3, sk next 5 sc on same petal of current shamrock, sc in next s ch 3, picot, ch 3, sk first 7 sc on stem, sc in next sc, ch 3 picot, ch 3; join with sl st in first sc: 9 picots and 1 joine picot. Finish off; weave in ends.

Additional Shamrocks

Work same as Second Shamrock, joining each shamroc previous shamrock, for desired length of edging.

Edging

Row 1 (wrong side): With wrong side facing and stem facing top, join with sl st in 3rd picot before joined picot First Shamrock, ch 11 (counts as tr and ch-7 sp), sc in n picot on same shamrock; *ch 11, work tr dec in next pic on same shamrock and in 3rd picot before joined picot o next shamrock, ch 11, sc in next picot on same shamroc rep from * across to last shamrock; ch 7, tr in next picot last shamrock; ch 4 (counts as dc and ch-1 sp on followi row), turn: 2 ch-sps across each shamrock.

Row 2 (right side): Sk next ch, dc in next ch; *ch 1, sk next ch, dc in next ch or st; rep from * across, working l dc in 4th ch of beg ch-11 on Row 1: 12 ch-1 sps across ea shamrock in center and 10 ch-1 sps across first and last shamrocks. Finish off; weave in ends.

Finishing

Wash and block. If desired, weave ribbon through space in Row 2 of edging; secure ends.

Flower Edging

Skill Level: Intermediate ■■■□

Finished Size: Approx. $4\frac{1}{4}$" (10.7 cm) wide x desir length

Materials:
Size 10 crochet thread 🔟 *Lace*
[100% cotton, 400 yards (365 meters)] per ball
1 ball white
Note: *Photographed model made with Aunt Lydia's®*
Classic Crochet Thread, size 10 #1 White.
Size 7 (1.65 mm) steel crochet hook (or size required for gauge)
Tapestry needle

Gauge: Rnds 1 and 2 of flower = 2" (5 cm) diameter

Stitch Guide

Small picot (sm picot): Ch 5, sl st in top of last st made before ch-5: sm picot made.

Large picot (lg picot): Ch 5, sl st in 5th ch from hook: lg picot made.

Picot join: Ch 2, sc in corresponding picot on previous flower, ch 2, sl st in top of last st made before first ch-2: picot join made.

Double treble crochet (dtr): YO 3 times, insert hook in specified st or sp and draw up a lp (5 lps on hook), [YO and draw through 2 lps on hook] 4 times: dtr made.

Note: *To join with sc, make a slip knot and place on hook, insert hook in specified st and draw up a lp, YO and draw through both lps on hook.*

Instructions

First Flower
Starting at center of flower, ch 9; join to form a ring.

Rnd 1 (right side): Ch 1, work 18 sc in ring; join with sl st in first sc: 18 sc.

Rnd 2: Ch 4, (2 tr, sm picot, 3 tr) in same sc as joining (petal made); *ch 1, lg picot, ch 2**, sk next 2 sc, (3 tr, sm picot, 3 tr) in next sc (petal made); rep from * around, ending last rep at **; join with sl st in 4th ch of beg ch-4: 6 petals and 12 picots. Finish off; weave in ends.

Rnd 3: With right side facing, join with sc in any lg picot, ch 15, [sc in next lg picot, ch 15] 5 times; join with sl st in first sc: 6 ch-lps.

Rnd 4: In each ch-lp around, work (5 sc, sm picot, [2 sc, sm picot] 4 times, 5 sc); join with sl st in first sc: 6 lps with 5 sm picots each. Finish off.

Second Flower

Rnds 1 through 3: Work same as Rnds 1 through 3 on First Flower.

Rnd 4: In each of first 4 ch-lps, work (5 sc, sm picot, [2 sc, sm picot] 4 times, 5 sc), in next ch-lp work (5 sc, [sm picot, 2 sc] 3 times, picot join to 2nd sm picot of 3rd lp on previous flower, 2 sc, picot join to first sm picot of same lp on previous flower, 5 sc), in last ch-lp work (5 sc, picot join to 5th sm picot of 2nd lp on previous flower, 2 sc, picot join to 4th sm picot of same lp on previous flower, [2 sc, sm picot] 3 times, 5 sc); join with sl st in first sc: 6 lps with 5 sm picots (or picot joins) each. Finish off.

Additional Flowers
Work same as Second Flower, joining each flower to previous flower, for desired length of edging.

Edging

Row 1: With right side facing, join with sl st in 5th sm picot of 3rd ch-lp on last flower, ch 17 (counts as dtr and ch-12 sp); *sc in 3rd sm picot of next ch-lp on same flower, ch 12, dtr in first sm picot of next ch-lp on same flower**, ch 9, dtr in 5th sm picot of 3rd ch-lp on next flower, ch 12; rep from * across, ending last rep at **; ch 1, turn: 2 ch-12 sps across each flower and 1 ch-9 lp between flowers.

Row 2: Sc in first dtr; *[(ch 4, sc) 4 times] in next ch-12 sp, ch 4, sc in next sc**, [(ch 4, sc) 4 times] in next ch-12 sp, ch 4, sc in next dtr, [(ch 4, sc) 3 times in next ch-9 sp, ch 4, sc in next dtr; rep from * across, ending last rep at **; [(ch 4, sc) 4 times] in beg ch-17 sp, ch 4, sc in 5th ch of beg ch-17: ch 4 (counts as dc and ch-1 sp on following row), turn: 10 ch-4 sps across each flower and 4 ch-4 sps between flowers.

Row 3: Hdc in next ch-4 sp; *ch 2, hdc in next ch-4 sp; rep from * across; ch 1, dc in last sc. Finish off; weave in ends.

Finishing
Wash and block.

Colleen Doily

Designed by Kathryn A. White

Skill Level: Intermediate ◼◼◻◻

Finished Size: Approx. 17"(43.18 cm) diameter

Materials:
Size 10 crochet thread ⓪ Lace
[100% cotton, 284 yards (259.7 meters)] per ball
    2 balls white
Note: *Photographed model made with DMC® Cebelia Crochet Cotton, size 10 #B5200 Bright White.*
Size 7 (1.65 mm) steel crochet hook (or size required for gauge)
Sizes H/8 (5 mm) and I/9 (5.5 mm) crochet hooks for making padding cord rings
Stitch marker

40

Gauge: Rnds 1 and 2 of center motif = 1¾ " (4.45 cm) diameter

Stitch Guide
Padding cord ring (pc ring): Leaving approx. 1" (2.54 cm) tail, wrap thread 8 to12 times around non-working end of specified crochet hook (the more wraps, the more 3-dimensional the pc ring will be). Cut thread, leaving approx. 1" (2.54 cm) tail. Gently slide wraps off hook and insert steel hook into ring. Pull working thread through ring, work specified number of sc in ring, as specified in pattern. **Hint:** *Do not wrap thread too tightly around hook or you will have trouble sliding wraps off hook and retaining their round shape.*

...dding cord (pc): A specified number of strands of thread (...pically 4 to 6 strands) that are crocheted over to provide (...pe and definition to a piece or motif. **Note:** *Be sure to ...ust the tension of the padding cord often.*

...ain-4 picot (ch-4 picot): Ch 4, sl st in top of last st ...de before ch-4: ch-4 picot made.

...reble crochet cluster (2-tr cl): *YO twice, insert hook ...ndicated ch or st and draw up a lp, [YO and draw ...ough 2 lps on hook] twice; rep from * once in same ch ...t; YO and draw through all lps on hook: 2-tr cl made.

...reble crochet cluster leaf (2-tr cl leaf): Ch 4, work 2-tr ...n 4th ch from hook, ch-4 picot, ch 4, sl st in ch at base of ...r cl: 2-tr cl leaf made.

...verse 2 treble crochet cluster leaf (rev 2-tr cl leaf): Ch ...work 2-tr cl in ch at base of first leaf, ch-4 picot, ch 4, sl ...n ch at base of 2-tr cl: rev 2-tr cl leaf made.

...side 2 treble crochet cluster leaf (inside 2-tr cl leaf): ...7, work 2-tr cl in 4th ch from hook, ch 1, sl st in ...cified ch-4 picot on flower, ch 1, sl st in top of cl just ...de, ch 4, sl st in ch at base of 2-tr cl, sl st around ch at ...e of leaf just made: inside 2-tr cl leaf made.

...tside 2 treble crochet cluster leaf (outside 2-tr cl ...f): Ch 7, work 2-tr cl in 4th ch from hook, ch-4 picot, ch ...rotate leaf, sl st in free lp of ch at base of leaf (this will ...sition leaf on opposite side of ch): outside 2-tr cl leaf ...de.

...ain-3 picot (ch-3 picot): Ch 3, sl st in top of last st ...de before ch-3: ch-3 picot made.

...iple Picot (tr picot): Ch 4, sl st in top of last st made ...st picot made), ch 5, sl st in same st, catching front lp of ...t picot (2nd picot made), ch 4, sl st in same st, catching ...nt lp of first and 2nd picots (3rd picot made): triple picot ...de.

...structions

...nter Motif
...t 3 pieces of size 10 thread, 22" (55.88 cm) long for pc. ...ld in half and set aside.
...t 3 pieces of size 10 thread, 24" (60.96 cm) long for pc. ...ld in half and set aside.

Rnd 1 (right side): Using non-working end of I hook, start pc ring. Ch 1, 2 sc in ring, ch 8, [4 sc in ring, ch 8] 5 times, 2 sc in ring; join with sl st in first sc and through fold of 22" pc: 6 ch-8 sps and 24 sc.

Rnd 2: Working over all 6 strands of pc, ch 1, sc in same st as joining, 5 sc in next ch-8 sp, [ch 3, sc in same ch-8 sp] 5 times, 4 sc in same ch-8 sp (petal made); *skip next sc, sc in next 2 sc, 5 sc in next ch-8 sp, ch 1, sl st in last ch-3 sp on previous petal**, working on current petal, [ch 3, sc in same ch-8 sp] 4 times, 4 sc in same ch-8 sp; rep from * around, ending last rep at **; working on current petal, [ch 3, sc in same ch-8 sp] 3 times, ch 1, sl st in first ch-3 sp on first petal, ch 1, 5 sc in same ch-8 sp on current petal, skip next sc, sc in next sc; join with sl st in first sc: 6 petals. Finish off; weave in ends.

Rnd 3: With right side facing, join with sl st in center ch-3 sp on any petal, ch 1, sc in same ch-3 sp, ch 10; *skip next 2 unjoined ch-3 sps, sc in next ch-3 sp, ch 10; rep from * around, ending last rep at **; join with sl st in first sc and through fold of 24" pc: 6 ch-10 sps.

Rnd 4: Working over all 6 strands of pc, ch 1; *sc in center ch-3 sp on Rnd 2 of petal, 4 sc in next ch-10 sp, [ch 3, 3 sc in same ch-10 sp] 2 times, ch 3, 4 sc in same ch-10 sp; rep from around; join with sl st in first sc: 18 ch-3 sps. Finish off; weave in ends.

Outer Motif #1
Cut 3 pieces of size 10 thread, 36"(91.44 cm) long for pc. Fold in half and set aside.

Flower
Rnd 1 (right side): Using non-working end of H hook, start pc ring. Ch 1, 16 sc in ring; join with sl st in front lp of first sc: 16 sc.

Rnd 2: Working in front lps only, ch 1, sc in same sc as joining, 5 dc in next sc; *sc in next sc, 5 dc in next sc; rep from * around; join with sl st in first sc: 8 petals.

Rnd 3: Working in back lps of Rnd 1, ch 1, sc in first sc (same sc as joining), ch 3, skip next sc; *sc in next sc, ch 3; rep from * around; join with sl st in first sc: 8 ch-3 sps.

Rnd 4: *(Sl st, ch 2, 3 dc, ch-4 picot, 2 dc, ch 3, sl st) in next ch-3 sp; rep from * around; join with sl st in first sl st: 8 petals. Finish off; weave in ends.

Instructions continued on page 42

Leaf Vine

Starting with slip knot on hook, [work 2-tr cl leaf] twice, sl st around ch at base of 2nd leaf, sl st in ch at base of first leaf, work rev 2-tr cl leaf, work inside 2-tr cl leaf, joining tip of leaf to any ch-4 picot on flower, work outside 2-tr cl leaf, [work inside 2-tr cl leaf, joining tip of leaf to next ch-4 picot on flower, work outside 2-tr cl leaf] 2 times, work inside 2-tr cl leaf, joining tip of leaf to same ch-4 picot on flower, work outside 2-tr cl leaf, work inside 2-tr cl leaf, joining tip of leaf to next ch-4 picot on flower, work rev 2-tr cl leaf in same ch at base of previous leaf, sl st around ch at base of previous leaf; place marker in picot on leaf just made; work outside 2-tr cl leaf, work inside 2-tr cl leaf, joining tip of leaf to next ch-4 picot on flower, work outside 2-tr cl, work inside 2-tr cl, joining tip of leaf to same ch-4 picot on flower, [work outside 2-tr cl leaf, work inside 2-tr cl leaf, joining tip of leaf to next ch-4 picot on flower] 2 times, ch 3, [work 2-tr cl leaf] twice, sl st around ch at base of 2nd leaf, sl st in ch at base of first leaf, work rev 2-tr cl leaf: 24 2-tr cl leaves (including inside, outside and rev 2-tr cl leaves). Finish off; weave in ends.

8-Pointed Ring

Rnd 1 (right side): Using non-working end of H hook, start pc ring. Ch 1, sc in ring, ch 3, 2 sc in ring] 7 times, ch 1, sl st in picot of marked leaf on Leaf Vine, ch 1 (joined ch-3 sp made), sc in ring; join with sl st in first sc: 7 ch-3 sps and 1 joined ch-3 sp. Finish off; weave in ends.

Motif Border

Rnd 1: With right side facing, join with sl st in free ch-4 picot on flower, ch 1, sc in same picot, ch 10, sc in picot on first free leaf, [ch 9, sc in picot on next leaf] 2 times, ch 5, [sc in picot on next leaf, ch 8] 3 times, dc in picot on next leaf, ch 5, sk first ch-3 sp on 8-Pointed Ring after join, sc in next ch-3 sp, [ch 2, sc in next ch-3 sp] 2 times, ch 5, sc in same ch-3 sp, [ch 2, sc in next ch-3 sp] 2 times, ch 5, dc in picot on next leaf, [ch 8, sc in picot on next leaf] 3 times, ch 5, sc in picot on next leaf, [ch 9, sc in picot on next leaf] 2 times, ch 10; join with sl st in first sc and through fold of 36" padding cord: 21 ch-sps.

Rnd 2: Working over all 6 strands of pc, ch 1, sc in same sc as joining, 12 sc in next ch-10 sp, [11 sc in next ch-9 sp] 2 times, 6 sc in next ch-5 sp, [10 sc in next ch-8 sp] 3 times, 5 sc in next ch-5 sp, [2 sc in next ch-2 sp] 2 times, 7 sc in next ch-5 sp, [2 sc in next ch-2 sp] 2 times, 5 sc in next ch-5 sp, [10 sc in next ch-8 sp] 3 times, 6 sc in next ch-5 sp, [11 sc in next ch-9 sp] 2 times, 12 sc in next ch-10 sp; join with sl st in first sc: 165 sc. Drop padding cord.

Rnd 3: Sl st in next sc, (sl st, ch 1, sc) in next sc, [ch 3 skip next 2 sc, sc in next sc] 27 times, ch 5, sc in same sc, [ch 3, skip next 2 sc, sc in next sc] 27 times, ch 1; join with sl st in first sc: 54 ch-3 sps, 1 ch-5 sp and 1 ch-1 sp

Rnd 4: Sl st in first ch-3 sp, ch 1, 3 sc in same ch-3 sp, sc, ch-3 picot, sc) in next ch-3 sp] 25 times, 3 sc in nex ch-3 sp, 3 sc in next ch-5 sp, ch 1, sl st in center ch-3 sp of 3 ch-3 sps on Rnd 4 of Center Motif that are worked any ch-10 sp on Rnd 3 of Center Motif, ch 1, 3 sc in sa ch-5 sp on Motif Border, 3 sc in next ch-3 sp, [(2 sc, ch picot, sc) in next ch-3 sp] 25 times, 3 sc in next ch-3 sp sc in next ch-1 sp; join with sl st in first sc: 50 ch-3 pic Finish off; weave in ends.

Outer Motifs # 2 to 5

Follow instructions for Outer Motif #1 until Rnd 3 of Motif Border is complete.

Rnd 4: Sl st in first ch-3 sp, ch 1, 3 sc in same ch-3 sp, [(2 sc, ch-3 picot, sc) in next ch-3 sp] 25 times, 3 sc in next ch-3 sp, 3 sc in next ch-5 sp, ch 1, skip next 2 ch-3 sps on Center Motif, sl st in next ch-3 sp (in center ch-3 sp of 3 ch-3 sps on Rnd 4 of Center Motif that are work in next ch-10 sp on Rnd 3 of Center Motif), ch 1, 3 sc i same ch-5 sp on Motif Border, 3 sc in next ch-3 sp, [(2 ch-3 picot, sc) in next ch-3 sp] 4 times, 2 sc in next ch-sp, ch 1, skip next 4 ch-3 picots on previous Outer Mo after joining to Center Motif, sl st in next ch-3 picot, ch 1, sl st in last sc made on current motif (joined ch-3 pic made), sc in same ch-3 sp, [2 sc in next ch-3 sp, ch 1, sl in next picot on previous motif, ch 1, sl st in last sc mad on current motif (joined ch-3 picot made), sc in same ch-3 sp] 7 times, [(2 sc, ch-3 picot, sc) in next ch-3 sp] times, 3 sc in next ch-3 sp, sc in next ch-1 sp; join with sl st in first sc: 42 ch-3 picots and 8 joined picots. Finis off; weave in ends.

Outer Motif # 6

Follow instructions for Outer Motif #1 until Rnd 3 of Motif Border is complete.

Rnd 4: Sl st in first ch-3 sp, ch 1, 3 sc in same ch-3 sp, [(2 sc, ch-3 picot, sc) in next ch-3 sp] 13 times, 2 sc in next ch-3 sp, ch 1, skip next 13 picots from center on Outer Motif #1, sl st in next picot on Outer Motif #1, ch 1, sl st in last sc made on current motif (joined ch-3 picot made), sc in same ch-3 sp, [2 sc in next ch-3 sp, c 1, sl st in next picot on Outer Motif #1, ch 1, sl st in las sc made on current motif (joined ch-3 picot made), sc in

ne ch-3 sp] 7 times, [(2 sc, ch-3 picot, sc) in next ch-3
4 times, 3 sc in next ch-3 sp, 3 sc in next ch-5 sp, ch
skip next 2 ch-3 sps on Center Motif, sl st in next ch-3
(in center ch-3 sp of 3 ch-3 sps on Rnd 4 of Center
otif that are worked in next ch-10 sp on Rnd 3 of Center
otif), ch 1, 3 sc in same ch-5 sp, 3 sc in next ch-3 sp,
 sc, ch-3 picot, sc) in next ch-3 sp] 4 times, 2 sc in next
-3 sp, ch 1, skip next 4 ch-3 picots on Outer Motif #5,
 st in next ch-3 picot, ch 1, sl st in last sc made on
rrent motif (joined ch-3 picot made), sc in same ch-3
 [2 sc in next ch-3 sp, ch 1, sl st in next picot on Outer
otif #5, ch 1, sl st in last sc made on current motif
ined ch-3 sp made), sc in same ch-3 sp] 7 times, [(2
 ch-3 picot, sc) in next ch-3 sp] 13 times, 3 sc in next
-3 sp, sc in next ch-1 sp; join with sl st in first sc: 34
-3 picots and 16 joined ch-3 picots. Finish off; weave in
ds.

Petal Motifs Between Outer Motifs (make 6)

te: *Work one 6-Petal Motif between each 2 joined
ter Motifs.*

t 3 pieces of size 10 thread, 24" (60.96 cm) long for pc.
ld in half and set aside.

d 1 (right side): Using non-working end of I hook,
rt pc ring. Ch 1, 2 sc in ring, ch 8, [4 sc in ring, ch 8]
imes, 2 sc in ring; join with sl st in first sc and through
d of 24" pc: 6 ch-8 sps and 24 sc.

d 2: Working over all 6 strands of pc, ch 1, sc in same
 as joining, 5 sc in next ch-8 sp, [ch 3, sc in same ch-8
 2 times, tr picot, [sc in same ch-8 sp, ch 3] 2 times, 5
 in same ch-8 sp (petal made), [skip next sc, sc in next
c, 5 sc in next ch-8 sp, ch 1, sl st in last ch-3 sp on
evious petal, ch 1, sc in same ch-8 sp, ch 3, sc in same
-8 sp, tr picot, (sc in same ch-8 sp, ch 3) 2 times, 5 sc
 same ch-8 sp (petal made)] 2 times, skip next sc, sc in
xt 2 sc, 5 sc in next ch-8 sp, ch 1, sl st in last ch-3 sp on
evious petal, ch 1, sc in same ch-8 sp, ch 3, sc in same
-8 sp, ch 1, sl st in 10th ch-3 picot from center of Outer
otif, ch 1, [sc in same ch-8 sp, ch 3] 2 times, 5 sc in
ne ch-8 sp (petal made), skip next sc, sc in next 2 sc,
c in next ch-8 sp, ch 1, sl st in last ch-3 sp on previous
tal, ch 1, sc in same ch-8 sp, ch 3, sc in same ch-8 sp, tr
:ot, [sc in same ch-8 sp, ch 3] 2 times, 5 sc in same ch-8
(petal made), skip next sc, sc in next 2 sc, 5 sc in

next ch-8 sp, ch 1, sl st in last ch-3 sp on previous petal,
ch 1, sc in same ch-8 sp, ch 3, sc in same ch-8 sp, ch 1,
skip next 6 ch-3 picots (3 picots on same Outer Motif and
3 picots on next Outer Motif), sl st in next picot of next
Outer Motif (in 10th ch-3 picot from center of next Outer
Motif), ch 1, sc in same ch-8 sp, ch 3, sc in same ch-8 sp,
ch 1, sl st in first ch-3 sp on first petal, ch 1, 5 sc in same
ch-8 sp (petal made), skip next sc, sc in next sc; join with
sl st in first sc: 6 petals (2 joined petals and 4 unjoined
petals). Finish off; weave in ends.

Edging

Cut 3 pieces of size 10 thread, 4 yards (3.65 meters) long
for pc. Fold in half and set aside.

Rnd 1 (right side): With right side facing, join in center
lp of first unworked tr picot of 3 unworked tr picot on any
6-Petal Motif, ch 1, sc in same lp; *[ch 8, sc in center lp
of next tr picot] 2 times, ch 4, sk next picot on next Outer
Motif, dc in next picot, [ch 4, dc in next picot] 7 times, ch
1, dc in next picot, [ch 4, dc in next picot] 7 times, ch 4**,
sc in center lp of next tr picot on next 6-Petal Motif; rep
from * around, ending last rep at **; join with sl st in first
sc: 114 ch-sps.

Rnd 2: (Sl st, ch 1, 8 sc) in first ch-8 sp, ch 2, turn; *skip
next 3 sc, (dc, ch 2, dc) in next sc, ch 2, sk next 2 sc, sc in
next sc, sl st in next sc, ch 1, turn; [(2 sc, ch-3 picot, sc) in
next ch-2 sp] 3 times, 4 sc in same ch-8 sp, sc in next sc,
3 sc in next ch-8 sp, ch 3, turn; skip next 3 sc, (tr, ch 3, tr)
in next sc, ch 3, skip next 2 sc, sc in next sc, sl st in next
sc, ch 1, turn; (3 sc, ch-3 picot, 2 sc) in next ch-3 sp, (3
sc, tr picot, 2 sc) in next ch-3 sp, (3 sc, ch-3 picot, 2 sc) in
next ch-3 sp, 7 sc in same ch-8 sp, ch 2, turn; skip next 3
sc, (dc, ch 2, dc) in next sc, ch 2, skip next 2 sc, sc in next
sc, sl st in next sc, ch 1, turn; [(2 sc, ch-3 picot, sc) in next
ch-2 sp] 3 times, sc in same ch-8 sp, [(3 sc, ch-3 picot, 2
sc) in next ch-4 sp] 7 times, 4 sc in next ch-4 sp, sc in next
ch-1 sp, 3 sc in next ch-4 sp, ch 5, turn; skip next 6 sc, sc
in next sc, sl st in next sc, ch 1, turn; (5 sc, tr picot, 4 sc)
in next ch-5 sp, sc in same ch-4 sp, [(3 sc, ch-3 picot, 2
sc) in next ch-4 sp] 7 times**, 8 sc in next ch-8 sp, ch 2,
turn; rep from * around, ending last rep at **; with sl st in
first sc: 12 tr picots and 132 picots. Finish off; weave in
ends.

Finishing
Wash and block.

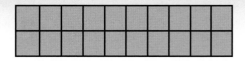
FILET CROCHET

Filet crochet is a technique that allows you to create beautiful designs with easy basic stitches. It is formed with squares, some open, and some closed, called closed mesh and open mesh (or sometimes blocks and spaces). It is worked by following charts, which are much easier to follow than written instructions.

How To Do Filet Crochet

Here is a close-up photo of an actual filet piece, which shows the structure of the design.

And here is the chart that was used to work the piece. You can see that the chart is almost the exact image of the actual worked piece.

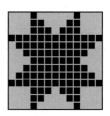

Reading the Charts

On our charts, a blank square stands for a space or an open mesh, and a filled-in square stands for a block or a closed mesh.

An open mesh (or space) is made with a dc, then 2 chs, then another dc.

The chart for open meshes (spaces) will look like this:

To start a row of open mesh, form the first dc and ch-2 sp by working a ch 5 at the end of the preceding row. This ch 5 equals a dc and a ch-2 sp. To end the row, work the final dc into the third ch of the ch-5 turning ch.

A closed mesh (block) is made by 4 dc sts: one on each side and 2 in the middle. To work a closed mesh over an open mesh on the previous row, work: dc in next dc, 2 dc in ch-2 sp, dc in next dc. To work a closed mesh over a closed mesh on the previous row, work: dc in next 4 dc.

A chart showing closed meshes will look like this:

To start a row of closed mesh, form the first dc by working a ch 3 at the end of the preceding row. This ch 3 equals a dc. To end the row, work the final dc into the third ch of the ch-3 turning ch.

Note: *The last dc of each mesh is shared with the first d of the following mesh in the row.*

Increasing and Decreasing

In some designs, you will be increasing or decreasing th number of closed meshes or open meshes at the edges.

Increases in Open Mesh
Increases are made by working additional chs, as specif in the pattern, in the turning ch at the end of a row to ad blocks for the next row.

Before turning row   After turning row

To add open meshes at the beginning of the next row, cl before turning for the next row, then work a dc in the fir dc of the previous row.

To add open meshes at the end of the working row, wo a ch 2, then a double triple crochet (YO 3 times) in the same place as last dc was made.

reases in Closed Mesh

dd closed mesh at the beginning of the next row, ch
fore turning for the next row. At the beginning of the
t (increase) row, dc in 5th and 6th chain from hook and
rst dc of previous row.

add closed mesh at the end of the row, triple crochet
he same chain of the turning chain as last double
chet made; (triple crochet in the base of last triple
chet made) twice.

creases

creases at the beginning of a row are worked by
ing without chaining. Then skip the first dc of the
vious row, sl st across each chain and in each dc until
reach the first block that will be worked; chain 5,
the next 2 stitches or chains, double crochet in the
t double crochet.

ecrease at the end of a row is made by working the
block shown on the chart, then turning, leaving the
owing blocks unworked.

Lacets

A lacet is a decorative stitch that is shown on the charts
by this symbol.

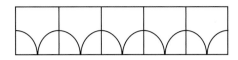

A lacet covers two open meshes or two closed meshes
and two rows, and is worked like this: Dc in next dc, ch
3, skip next 2 sts, sc in next st, ch 3, skip next 2 sts, dc in
next st.

To work the next row above a lacet: dc in first dc of
lacet, ch 5, dc in next dc.

Working from the Charts
The first row of each chart is read from right to left,
the second row from left to right. Continue alternating
directions with each row.

Quilt Block Filet Pillow

Designed by Susan Lowman
for Red Heart®

ill Level: Intermediate ■■■□

nished Size: Approx. 18" x 18" (45.7 cm x 45.7 cm)

aterials:
10 crochet thread
0% cotton, 350 yards (320 meters)] per ball
balls copper

te: Photographed model made with Aunt Lydia's®
ssic Crochet Thread, size 10 #310 Copper Mist.

7 (1.65 mm) steel crochet hook (or size required for
auge)
x 18" premade pillow (or 18" x 18" pillow form and
yard of 44" wide fabric)
ving needle
tching sewing thread
estry needle

auge: 12 blocks/mesh = 4" (10 cm)
12 rows = 4" (10 cm)

tch Guide

tended double crochet (edc): YO, insert hook in
cified st and draw up a lp, YO and draw through one lp
hook, [YO and draw through 2 lps on hook] twice: edc
de.

ck: Edc in next 3 sts: block made.

sh: Ch 2, sk next 2 sts, edc in next st: mesh made.

Instructions
Ch 163.

Row 1 (right side): Edc in 5th ch from hook (4 skipped chs count as first edc), edc in next ch and in each rem ch across: 160 edc; ch 3 (counts as first edc on next row now and throughout), turn.

Row 2: Edc in next 3 sts (block made); *ch 2, sk next 2 sts, edc in next st (mesh made); rep from * across to last 3 sts; work block; 2 blocks and 51 mesh; ch 3, turn.

Rows 3 through 53: Work blocks and mesh as per chart. At end of Rows 3 through 52, ch 3, turn. At end of Row 53, ch 1, do not turn.

Edging:
Work 3 sc in top of last edc on Row 53 (corner made), work 2 sc around post of last edc on Row 53, work 3 sc evenly spaced across edge of each rem row across side edge; working across opposite side of foundation ch, 3 sc in first ch (corner made), sc in each rem ch across to last ch, 3 sc in last ch (corner made); working across next side edge, work 3 sc evenly spaced across edge of each row across side edge; working across sts on Row 53, 3 sc in first st (corner made), sc in each st across to first corner; join with sl st in first sc. Finish off; weave in ends.

Finishing:
Wash and block crocheted piece to 18" (45.72 cm) square. Allow to dry completely.

Pillow Form Cover (optional):
Note: *If you are using a premade pillow, this step is not required.*
Cut fabric into 2 pieces, each measuring 19" x 19" (48.26 cm x 48.26 cm) square. With right sides of fabric together, sew 3 sides together, with ½" seam allowance. Turn piece right side out. Insert pillow form, and sew last side closed, using any hidden or invisible stitch desired.

Assembly:
Pin edges of crocheted piece to edges of pillow front. Sew edges of crocheted piece to edges of pillow with sewing needle and matching thread.

Home Sweet Home Wall Hanging

Skill Level: Intermediate ■■■□

Finished Size: Approx. 31" wide x 24 ½" high

Materials:
Cotton crochet thread, size 20 [0 Lace]
[100% cotton, 400 yards (365 meters)] per ball
  4 balls natural
Note: *Photographed model made with Aunt Lydia's® Fine Crochet Thread, size 20 #226 Natural.*

Size 10 (1.3mm) steel crochet hook (or size required for gauge)
¼" (.635 cm) diameter wooden dowel, 33" (83.82 cm) long
2 finial caps with ¼" hole
Fine sandpaper (optional)
Wood glue (optional)
Spray Starch (optional)
Tapestry needle

Gauge: 16 mesh = 4" (10.16 cm); 16 mesh rows = 4" (10.16 cm)(blocked)

ck: Dc in next 3 dc (or 2 dc in next ch-2 sp, dc in next
: block made.

sh: Ch 2, sk next 2 dc (or next ch-2 sp), dc in next dc.

structions
371.

ndation Row (wrong side): Sc in 2nd ch from hook
in each rem ch across: 370 sc; ch 3 (counts as dc on
t row now and throughout), turn.

w 1 (right side): *Dc in next 3 sc (block made); rep
m * across: 123 blocks; ch 3, turn.

w 2: Dc in next 3 dc (block made); *ch 2, sk next 2 dc,
in next dc; rep from * across, working last dc in 3rd ch
urning ch-3: 2 blocks and 121 mesh; ch 3, turn.

ws 3 through 101: Follow chart, working blocks and
sh as per instructions, working last dc of each row in
ch of turning ch-3. Ch 3, turn at end of Rows 3 through
. At end of Row 101, ch 1, turn.

Row 102: Sc in each dc across, working last sc in top of
turning ch-3: 370 sc; ch 10, turn.

Row 103: Sk next sc; *sc in next 3 sc, ch 10, sk next sc;
rep from * across, ending with sc in next 3 sc, ch 10, sc in
last sc: 93 ch-10 lps. Finish off; weave in ends.

Finishing
Wash and block. Allow to dry. If desired, spray with a
commercial spray starch until wet. Let dry thoroughly.

Hanging
If needed, sand dowel until smooth. Insert dowel through
ch-10 hanging loops at top of piece, carefully sliding
loops along dowel. Insert finial caps on ends of dowel.
You may glue the finial caps in place, if desired. But
if you leave the finial caps loose, the hanging can be
removed from the dowel at a later time to wash it when
it gets dirty or dusty! Make a chain approx. 36" long for
hanging piece. Tie ends of chain around groove in each
finial cap. Weave in ends.

POLISH STARS

Polish Stars is an intriguing crochet technique that looks much harder than it actually is. The Polish Star originated in Poland as a symbol of hope. The technique was not introduced into the United States until the later part of the twentieth century.

How To Do Polish Stars

Crocheted Polish Stars are worked in rows with 1 color of yarn used per row and 2 (or more) colors throughout the design (typically a dark color and a light color for contrast). Chain loops are made in most of the single-colored rows, according to the pattern, and woven in a particular order to form the Polish Stars. The chain loops are not worked into later on in the usual manner of working crochet in chain loops or chain spaces. The chain loops dangle on the right side of the work and are made for weaving together to form the Polish Stars on the right side. The instructions in each Polish Star pattern tells how to weave the chain loops to form the stars.

To create the Polish Stars, the chain loops are crossed in pairs across the specified row, according to the pattern. Then the loops in the row above are inserted into these crossed loops. Typically, the loops on the dark colored rows are crossed and the loops on the light colored rows are inserted into the dark colored loops one row below without crossing the light colored loops. After this, the dark colored loops in the next row above are inserted into the light colored loops below and the dark colored loops are crossed again, alternating where the loops are crossed to create staggered stars in the piece. This leaves one loop at the beginning and one loop at the end of every other dark colored row uncrossed. Inserting and crossing the loops is done in rows, starting at the botto of the piece and working up to the top. The loops can inserted and crossed at regular intervals while working the piece or all of the inserting and crossing can be do after the last row of loops has been worked. After all t loops are inserted and crossed, the loops in the top rov are secured in place by working a row of stitches acro the top of the piece, catching the last row of loops in t row of stitches, per the instructions in the pattern. It is the combination of inserting loops and crossing loops that forms the star shape of the Polish Stars.

The looping diagram looks something like this in Poli Stars patterns:

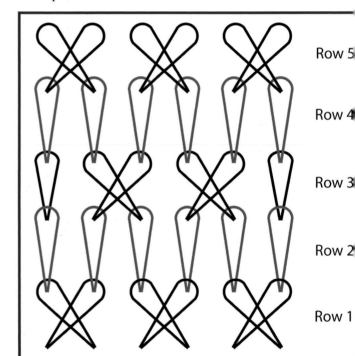

Row 5

Row 4

Row 3

Row 2

Row 1

Polish Stars Poncho

Designed by
Susan Lowman for
Red Heart®

Skill Level: Intermediate ■■■□

Finished Size: 30" (76.2 cm) neck circumference, [1]" (45.72 cm) long at sides and 23" (58.42 cm) long at [po]ints, plus 3" (3.75 cm) fringe

Materials:

Worsted weight yarn [4] Medium

[1]00% acrylic, 7 ounces, 364 yards (198 grams, 333 [me]ters)] per skein

2 skeins dark blue
2 skeins light blue
3 skeins white
Size I/9 (5.5 mm) crochet hook or size required for gauge
Note: *Photographed model made with Red Heart® Super Saver® #380 Windsor Blue, #382 Country Blue and #316 Soft White.*
Tapestry needle
Stitch markers

Instructions continue on page 52

Gauge: 14 edc = 4" (10 cm)
6 rows = 4" (10 cm)

Stitch Guide

Extended double crochet (edc): YO, insert hook in indicated st and draw up a lp, YO and draw through one lp on hook, (YO and draw through 2 lps on hook) twice: edc made.

Join with edc: Make a slip knot and place it on hook. YO, insert hook in indicated st and draw up a lp, YO and draw through one lp on hook; (YO and draw through 2 lps on hook) twice: join with edc made.

Double crochet decrease (dc dec): YO, insert hook in first indicated st and draw up a lp, YO and draw through 2 lps on hook; YO, insert hook in next indicated st and draw up a lp, YO and draw through 2 lps on hook; YO and draw through all 3 lps on hook: dc dec made.

3 double crochet decrease (3-dc dec): (YO, insert hook in next st and draw up a lp, YO and draw through 2 lps on hook) 3 times; YO and draw through all 4 lps on hook: 3-dc dec made.

3-single crochet decrease (3-sc dec): Insert hook in first indicated st and draw up a lp, insert hook in 2nd indicated st and draw up a lp, insert hook in 3rd indicated st and draw up a lp; YO and draw through all 4 lps on hook: 3-sc dec made.

Note: *Keep loops on right side of pieces throughout.*

Instructions

Square A (make 2)
With dark blue, ch 49.

Row 1 (wrong side): Sc in 2nd ch from hook, sc in next ch, (ch 12, sl st in top of last sc, sc in next 4 chs) 11 times, ch 12, sl st in top of last sc, sc in last 2 chs; turn: 48 sc and 12 ch-12 lps. Finish off.

Row 2 (right side): Join white with edc in first st, 2 edc in next sc, ch 10, sl st in top of last edc, (*sk next sc, edc in next 2 sc, ch 10, sl st in top of last edc, sk next sc, 2 edc in next sc*, edc in next 2 sc, 2 edc in next sc, ch 10, sl st in top of last edc) 5 times; rep from * to * once; edc in last sc; turn: 48 edc and 12 ch-10 lps. Finish off.

Row 3: Join dark blue with edc in first edc, edc in next edc, ch 10, sl st in top of last edc, (*sk next edc, 2 edc in

52

each of next 2 edc*; ch 12; **sl st in top of last edc, sk next edc**; edc in next 4 edc, ch 12, sl st in top of last edc) 5 times; rep from * to * once; ch 10; rep from ** to ** once; edc in last 2 edc; turn: 48 edc, 10 ch-12 lps and 2 ch-10 lps. Finish off.

Looping (6 Star Row): After working Row 3, insert 2nd blue lp from right 2 rows below (on Row 1) through first blue lp on right 2 rows below (on Row 1) and cross lps (2nd lp becomes first lp and first lp becomes 2nd lp after crossing lps). Insert (but do not cross) first white lp one row below (on Row 2) through first blue lp 2 rows below (on Row 1) and 2nd white lp one row below (on Row 2) through 2nd blue lp 2 rows below (on Row 1). Continue in same manner with next pair of 2 lps, 5 times more across rows: 6 crossed blue lps/Polish Stars on Row 1.

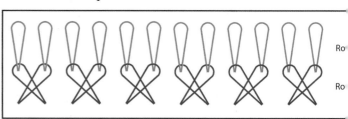

Row 4: Join white with edc in first edc, (*ch 10, sl st in top of last edc, sk next edc, 2 edc in next edc, edc in next 2 edc, 2 edc in next edc, ch 10, sl st in top of last edc, sk next edc*; edc in next 2 edc) 5 times; rep from * to * once; edc in last edc; turn: 48 edc and 12 ch-10 lps. Finish off.

Row 5: Join dark blue with edc in first edc, edc in same edc, (*ch 12, sl st in top of last edc, sk next edc, edc in next 4 edc, ch 12, sl st in top of last edc, sk next edc*; **2 edc in next edc; rep from ** once) 5 times; rep from * to * once; 2 edc in last edc; turn: 48 edc and 12 ch-12 lps. Finish off.

Looping (5 Star Row): After working Row 5 (and Rows 9, 13, 17 and 21), insert (but do not cross) each of 12 blue lps 2 rows below through each of 12 white lps 3 rows directly below. Insert (but do not cross) first white lp on right one row below through first blue lp on right 2 rows below. Insert 3rd blue lp from right 2 rows below through 2nd blue lp from right 2 rows below and cross lps (3rd lp becomes 2nd lp and 2nd lp becomes 3rd lp after crossing lps). Insert (but do not cross) 2nd white lp one row below through 2nd blue lp 2 rows below and 3rd white lp one row below through 3rd blue lp 2 rows below. Continue in same manner with next pair of 2 lps, 4 times more across rows. Insert last white lp one row below through last blue lp 2 rows below: 5 crossed blue lps/Polish Stars and 2 ending lps on Row 3.

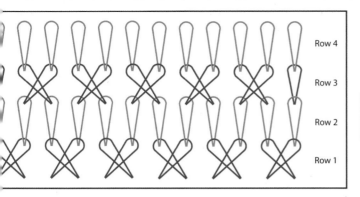

Row 4

Row 3

Row 2

Row 1

w 6: Join white with edc in first edc, 2 edc in next edc,
h 10, sl st in top of last edc, sk next edc, edc in next
dc, ch 10, sl st in top of last edc, sk next edc, 2 edc in
xt edc*, edc in next 2 edc, 2 edc in next edc) 5 times;
 from * to * once; edc in last edc; turn: 48 edc and 12
10 lps. Finish off.

ws 7 through 22: Rep Rows 3 through 6 four times
re, using dark blue for Rows 7, 17, 19 and 21, light
e for Rows 9, 11, 13 and 15 and white for all even
mbered rows.

oping (6 Star Row): After working Row 7 (and Rows
15, 19 and 23), insert (but do not cross) each of 12
e lps 2 rows below through each of 12 white lps 3 rows
ectly below. Insert 2nd blue lp from right 2 rows below
ough first blue lp on right 2 rows below and cross lps
d lp becomes first lp and first lp becomes 2nd lp after
ssing lps). Insert (but do not cross) first white lp one
 below through first blue lp 2 rows below and 2nd
ite lp one row below through 2nd blue lp 2 rows below.
ntinue in same manner with next pair of 2 lps, 5 times
re across rows: 6 crossed blue lps/Polish Stars on Row
Work looping after each odd numbered row through
 23, alternating 6 star row and 5 star row.

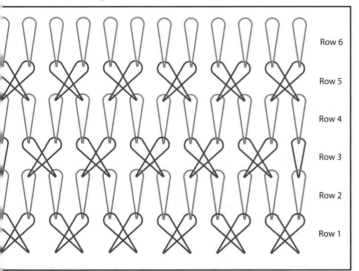

Row 6

Row 5

Row 4

Row 3

Row 2

Row 1

w 23: Rep Row 3.

Row 24: Join white with edc in first edc, (*sk next edc,
2 edc in next edc, edc in next 2 edc, 2 edc in next edc,
sk next edc*, edc in next 2 edc) 5 times; rep from * to *
once; edc in last edc; do not turn: 48 edc. Finish off.

Note: *Make sure all ch-lps have been properly inserted
and crossed before working Row 25.*

Row 25: With right side facing, join dark blue with sc in
first edc, (*insert hook through next lp and sc in next edc, sc
in next 4 edc*; make sure next 2 lps are inserted and crossed,
insert hook through next lp and sc in next edc, sc in next 2
edc) 5 times; rep from * to * once; insert hook through next
lp and sc in next edc; sc in last edc: 48 sc. Finish off.

Square B (make 2)
With light blue, ch 49. Rep Rows 1 through 25 of Square
A, using light blue for Rows 1, 3, 5, 7, 17, 19, 21, 23 and
25, dark blue for Rows 9, 11, 13 and 15 and white for all
even numbered rows.

Square Edging

With right side facing, join same blue as Row 1 with sc in
edge of last sc in Row 1 at bottom right corner, working
up right edge, work 2 sc around post of edc on edge of
each row and one sc in edge of sc in Row 25 at top right
corner: 48 sc. Finish off.

With right side facing, work left edge same as right edge
starting in last sc in Row 25 at top left corner and ending
in first sc in Row 1 at bottom left corner: 48 sc. Do not
finish off.

Rnd 1: Work 2 sc in free lp of ch where first sc on Row
1 is worked, sc in free lp of next 46 chs, 2 sc in free lp of
last ch; work rem 3 sides as follows: 2 sc in first sc, sc in
next 46 sc, 2 sc in last sc; sl st in first sc on bottom edge:
200 sc. Finish off.

Rnd 2: With right side facing, join white with sc in 2nd sc
on Rnd 1; *sc in back lp of next sc, sc in both lps of next
sc; rep from * 23 times more; **sc in back lp of same sc
as last sc made (place marker in this sc), sc in both lps
of next sc; rep from ** once; rep from * 3 times more,
omitting last sc in 3rd rep; sl st in first sc: 208 sc. Finish
off, leaving a long end for joining.

Finishing
Arrange squares as shown in photograph or as desired.
Whip stitch edges together through back lps only. Remove
all stitch markers except two at each bottom corner of
poncho.

Instructions continued on page 54

Bottom Border

With right side facing, join white with sc at center of one long side of poncho in both lps of a sc in Rnd 2 of square edging that was worked in back lp only; *sc in back lp of next sc that was worked in both lps, sc in both lps of next sc that was worked in back lp only; rep from * to square joining, working hdc in last unjoined st on current square; dc dec in next joined st of current square and in next joined st of next square; hdc in back lp of next unjoined st on next square; work sc in each st as before to bottom corner; in bottom corner work sc in both lps of first marked sc, sc in back lp of same sc, sc in both lps of next marked sc, sc in back lp of same sc, work sc in each st along next side and square joinings as before, work next bottom corner as before, work sc in each st along first side and square joining as before; join with sl st in first sc: 320 sts. Finish off.

Neck Border

Rnd 1: With right side facing, join white with sc at center of one side of one square in both lps of a sc in Rnd 2 of square edging that was worked in back lp only; *sc in back lp of next sc that was worked in both lps, sc in both lps of next sc that was worked in back lp only; rep from * to corner; hdc in last unjoined sc; work 3-dc dec in next 3 joined sts where 3 squares are joined; hdc in next unjoined st on next square; work sc as before along side of next square; work next corner as before, work sc as before along side of first square; join with sl st in first sc. Do not finish off.

Rnd 2: Ch 2, hdc in next sc, (hdc in each sc to corner; work 3-sc dec in next hdc, 3-dc dec and hdc) 2 times, hdc in each sc to beg; join with sl st in 2nd ch of beg ch-2. Finish off.

Fringe

With right side facing, join white with sl st in any st on bottom border, ch 25, sl st in next st, ch 15, drop white, join dark blue with sl st in next st, working behind dropped white ch-15 lp, ch 25, sl st in next st, ch 15, dro dark blue; *pick up white, working in front of dark blue ch-25 lp and behind dropped dark blue ch-15 lp, sl st in next st, ch 25, sl st in next st, ch 15, drop white; pick up dark blue, working in front of white ch-25 lp and behind dropped white ch-15 lp, sl st in next st, ch 25, sl st in nex st, ch 15, drop dark blue; rep from * around; join dark blue with sl st in beg white sl st and join dark blue with sl st in beg dark blue sl st. Finish off. Weave in ends.

Drawstring

With dark blue, make a chain 58" (147.32 cm) long. Weave in and out between hdc sts on Rnd 2 of neck border.

TAPESTRY CROCHET

Tapestry Crochet is a technique for creating a patterned [cloth] with 2 or more colors, switched back and forth, in [row] or round. Single crochet stitches are used, working [over] the yarn or thread colors that are currently not in [use] until these colors are needed again. Depending upon [the] tension and the number of yarns used, the finished [fabric] can be stiff or supple. Tapestry crochet has the [flex]ibility and portability of crochet, but it often does not [look] crocheted. In fact, the surface looks so much like [woven] fabric that many people think pieces worked with [tap]estry crochet were made on a loom.

[When] working the tapestry crochet stitch, insert the hook [from] front to back under the two top loops of the stitch. [The] carried thread is placed over the top of the stitches [and] is encased almost invisibly in the newly created [stit]ches. Use a hook with a handle, and—if possible— [hol]d it as if you were holding a knife. To keep the colors [from] tangling, put one to the left and the other to the [righ]t, allowing a twist to occur next to the stitch as the [col]ors are changed. Most tapestry crochet is done with [sin]gle crochet stitches, with the colors not in use carried [wit]hin the work. The designs are often worked from [cha]rts instead of written instructions.

How To Do Tapestry Crochet

Carrying Thread
[Pla]ce the thread to be carried over the top of the stitches [bein]g worked into, then single crochet across as usual, [enc]asing the carried thread between the stitches (Fig 1).

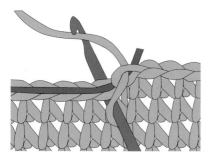

Fig 1

Changing Colors
Work a stitch until 2 loops remain on the hook; drop the working thread and pick up the non-working (carried) thread and draw through both loops on the hook. The previous non-working thread now becomes the working thread (Figs 2 and 3). The previous working thread now becomes the non-working thread and is carried over the top of the stitches in the row below.

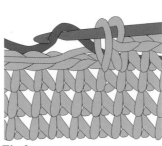
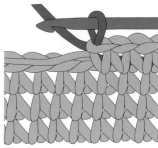

Fig 2   Fig 3

Tapestry Crochet Stitch
While carrying the non-working thread over stitches on the row below, insert the hook in the next stitch and draw up a loop with working thread, yarn over and draw through 2 loops on the hook, encasing the carried (non-working) thread between stitches (Fig 4).

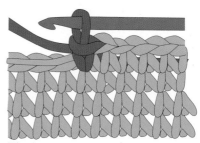

Fig 4

Adding or Discontinuing a Color
To add a new color, carry the new color for about 10 stitches, encasing it, before using it in the pattern. To end a color, complete the last stitch of the color to be discontinued and cut, leaving a short end to be carried and covered for about 10 stitches.

Tapestry Crochet Ornaments

Designed by Susan Lowman

Skill Level: Intermediate ■ ■ ■ □

Finished Size: Approx. 2" (5.1 cm) wide x 2½" (6.4 cm) high

Materials:

Size 3 crochet thread [100% cotton, 150 yards (137 meters)] per ball
  1 ball green, red (A)
  1 ball off-white, white (B)
  1 ball pink (C)
Cotton crochet thread, size 5 [93% mercerized cotton, 7% metallic filament, 100 yards (91 meters)] per ball
  1 ball gold (A) or (C), white (B), silver (C)

Note: *Photographed models made with Aunt Lydia's® Fashion Crochet, size 3 #625 Sage (A), # 6 Scarlet (A), #926 Bridal White (B), #201 White (B) #775 Warm Rose (Aunt Lydia's® Fashion Crochet Metallics, size 5 #90G Gold/Gold (A) or (C), #201P White/Pearl (B) and #41(Silver/Silver(C) .*

Size D/3 (3.25 mm) crochet hook or size required for gauge
Polyester fiberfill
Tapestry needle

Gauge: Gauge is not critical for these ornaments.

Stitch Guide

Single crochet decrease (sc dec): [Insert hook in next st and draw up a lp] twice, YO and draw through all 3 lps on hook: sc dec made.

Notes: Ornament is made in a spiral with unjoined rounds.

To work in Tapestry Crochet method, carry thread color not in use along top of stitches, encasing carried color under stitches until needed.

When changing colors, work last st until 2 lps rem on hook, drop old color to wrong side, pick up new color, YO and draw through 2 lps on hook. Continue working with new color until next color change.

Work last few stitches of old color over new color and work first few stitches of new color over old color to secure ends.

Instructions

Rnd 1 (right side): With A, ch 2, 6 sc in 2nd ch from hook: 6 sc.

Rnd 2: Start carrying C, 2 sc in each st around: 12 sc.

Rnd 3: Work [2 sc in next st, sc in next st] 6 times: 18 sc.

Rnd 4: Work [2 sc in next st, sc in next 2 sts] 6 times: 24 sc.

Rnd 5: Work [2 sc in next st, sc in next 3 sts] 6 times, changing to C in last st: 30 sc.

Rnd 6: With C, [2 sc in next st, sc in next 4 sts] 6 times, changing to B in last st: 36 sc.

Rnd 7: With B, sc in each st around.

Rnd 8: [With A, sc in next st, with B, sc in next 2 sts, 2 sc in next st, sc in next 2 sts] 6 times: 42 sc.

Rnd 9: [With A, sc in next 2 sts, with B, sc in next 5 sts] 6 times.

Rnd 10: [With A, sc in next 3 sts, with B, sc in next 4 sts] 6 times.

Rnd 11: [With A, sc in next 4 sts, with B, sc in next 3 sts] 6 times.

Rnd 12: [With A, sc in next 5 sts, with B, sc in next 2 sts] 6 times.

Rnd 13: [With A, sc in next 6 sts, with B, sc in next st] 6 times.

Rnd 14: [With A, sc in next 2 sts, sc dec in next 2 sts, sc in next 3 sts] 6 times, changing to C in last st: 36 sc.

Rnd 15: With C, sc in each st around, changing to B in last st.

Rnd 16: With B, [sc in next 4 sts, sc dec in next 2 sts] 6 times: 30 sc.

Rnd 17: [Sc in next 3 sts, sc dec in next 2 sts] 6 times: 24 sc.

Rnd 18: [Sc in next 2 sts, sc dec in next 2 sts] 6 times: 18 sc. Stuff firmly with fiberfill.

Rnd 19: [Sc in next st, sc dec in next 2 sts] 6 times: 12 sc.

Rnd 20: [Sc dec in next 2 sts] 6 times: 6 sc; join with sl st in next st. Finish off, leaving a 12" (30.48 cm) tail.

Finishing

Weave tail through stitches on Rnd 20 to close hole at top of ornament. Fold tail approx. 3" (7.62 cm) from top of ornament and tie a knot in doubled strand of tail at top of ornament to form hanging loop. Weave in remaining tail.

Tapestry
Crochet
Tote Bag

Designed by Susan Lowman

ill Level: Intermediate ■■■□

nished Size: Bag: Approx. 12"(30.5 cm) wide x
2" (29.2 cm) high x 2¾" (7 cm) deep
ndles: 18" (45.7 cm)

aterials:
 3
Light

rt weight yarn
0% cotton, 3.52 ounces, 218 yards (100 grams, 200
ers)] per ball
ball each: light green, dark green, light rust, dark rust,
ght tan, dark tan
te: *Photographed model made with Omega Sinfonia*
9 Light Olive, #889 Olive, #842 Cinnamon, #843 Dark
namon, #861 Sand and #863 Camel.
e E/4 (3.5 mm) crochet hook (or size required for
auge)
thesline: 9 to 10 yds (8.229 to 9.144 meters)
ric glue
ch markers
estry needle

auge: In tapestry crochet, 17 sc = 3" (7.62 cm)
ows = 3" (7.62 cm)

tch Guide
gle crochet decrease (sc dec): (Insert hook in next st
draw up a lp) twice; YO and draw through all 3 lps on
ok: sc dec made.

tes:
carry colors: *Lay non-working yarn over stitches on*
previous row, encasing carried yarn between sts.

change colors: *Work last st of old color until 2 lps*
on hook, drop old color and pick up new color from
rried colors, YO with new color and draw through 2 lps
hook. Continue with new color until next color change.

rried yarns can get bunched up when carrying them.
keep work smooth on wrong side, gently tug on carried
ns after every 5 to 10 stitches to keep them from
ching up under stitches.

structions

ttom
th dk green, ch 65.

w 1 (wrong side): Working in back bar of chs, sc in 2nd
from hook and in each rem ch across: 64 sc; ch 1, turn.

Rows 2 through 17: Sc in each sc across; ch 1, turn.

Edging
Work 3 sc in first sc, sc in next 62 sc, 3 sc in last sc;
working along left side, sc in edge of Rows 16 through 1;
working in free lps of foundation ch along bottom edge,
3 sc in first ch, sc in next 62 chs, 3 sc in last ch; working
along right side, sc in edge of Rows 1 through 16: 168 sc.
Do not join.

Sides
Rnd 1 (right side): Start to carry dk tan and dk rust,
ch 1, sc in same sc as joining and in each sc around.
Do not join.

Rnd 2: Sc in each sc around. Do not join.

Rnd 3: [With dk tan, sc in next sc, with lt green, sc in
next 12 sc, with dk rust, sc in next sc] 12 times.

Rnd 4: [With dk tan, sc in next 2 sc, with lt green, sc in
next 10 sc, with dk rust, sc in next 2 sc] 12 times.

Rnd 5: [With dk tan, sc in next 3 sc, with lt green, sc in
next 8 sc, with dk rust, sc in next 3 sc] 12 times.

Rnd 6: [With dk tan, sc in next 4 sc, with lt green, sc in
next 6 sc, with dk rust, sc in next 4 sc] 12 times.

Rnd 7: [With dk tan, sc in next 5 sc, with lt green, sc in
next 4 sc, with dk rust, sc in next 5 sc] 12 times.

Rnd 8: [With dk tan, sc in next 6 sc, with lt green, sc in
next 2 sc, with dk rust, sc in next 6 sc] 12 times.

Rnd 9: [With dk tan, sc in next 7 sc, with dk rust, sc in
next 7 sc] 12 times.

Rnd 10: [With dk green, sc in next sc, with dk tan, sc in
next 6 sc, with dk rust, sc in next 6 sc, with dk green, sc in
next sc] 12 times.

Rnd 11: [With dk green, sc in next 2 sc, with dk tan, sc in
next 5 sc, with dk rust, sc in next 5 sc, with dk green, sc in
next 2 sc] 12 times.

Rnd 12: [With dk green, sc in next 3 sc, with dk tan, sc in
next 4 sc, with dk rust, sc in next 4 sc, with dk green, sc in
next 3 sc] 12 times.

Instructions continued on page 60

Rnd 13: [With dk green, sc in next 4 sc, with dk tan, sc in next 3 sc, with dk rust, sc in next 3 sc, with dk green, sc in next 4 sc] 12 times.

Rnd 14: [With dk green, sc in next 5 sc, with dk tan, sc in next 2 sc, with dk rust, sc in next 2 sc, with dk green, sc in next 5 sc] 12 times.

Rnd 15: [With dk green, sc in next 6 sc, with dk tan, sc in next sc, with dk rust, sc in next sc, with dk green, sc in next 6 sc] 12 times.

Rnd 16: [With dk green, sc in next 6 sc, with lt rust, sc in next sc, with lt tan, sc in next sc, with dk green, sc in next 6 sc] 12 times.

Rnd 17: [With dk green, sc in next 5 sc, with lt rust, sc in next 2 sc, with lt tan, sc in next 2 sc, with dk green, sc in next 5 sc] 12 times.

Rnd 18: [With dk green, sc in next 4 sc, with lt rust, sc in next 3 sc, with lt tan, sc in next 3 sc, with dk green, sc in next 4 sc] 12 times.

Rnd 19: [With dk green, sc in next 3 sc, with lt rust, sc in next 4 sc, with lt tan, sc in next 4 sc, with dk green, sc in next 3 sc] 12 times.

Rnd 20: [With dk green, sc in next 2 sc, with lt rust, sc in next 5 sc, with lt tan, sc in next 5 sc, with dk green, sc in next 2 sc] 12 times.

Rnd 21: [With dk green, sc in next sc, with lt rust, sc in next 6 sc, with lt tan, sc in next 6 sc, with dk green, sc in next sc] 12 times.

Rnd 22: [With lt rust, sc in next 7 sc, with lt tan, sc in next 7 sc] 12 times.

Rnd 23: [With lt rust, sc in next 6 sc, with lt green, sc in next 2 sc, with lt tan, sc in next 6 sc] 12 times.

Rnd 24: [With lt rust, sc in next 5 sc, with lt green, sc in next 4 sc, with lt tan, sc in next 5 sc] 12 times.

Rnd 25: [With lt rust, sc in next 4 sc, with lt green, sc in next 6 sc, with lt tan, sc in next 4 sc] 12 times.

Rnd 26: [With lt rust, sc in next 3 sc, with lt green, sc in next 8 sc, with lt tan, sc in next 3 sc] 12 times.

Rnd 27: [With lt rust, sc in next 2 sc, with lt green, sc in next 10 sc, with lt tan, sc in next 2 sc] 12 times.

Rnd 28: [With lt rust, sc in next sc, with lt green, sc in next 12 sc, with lt tan, sc in next sc] 12 times.

Rnds 29 through 54: Rep Rnds 3 through 28.

Rnds 55 through 57: With dk green, rep Rnd 2, 3 times.

Rnd 58: Working over Rnd 57 into sc on Rnd 56, [sc next 12 sc, sc dec in next 2 sc] 12 times; join with sl st first sc: 156 sc. Finish off; weave in ends.

Handles (make 2)
With lt green, ch 105.

Rnd 1 (right side): Working in back bar of chs, sc in 2nd ch from hook and in each ch across to last ch, 5 sc in last ch (place marker in first sc of 5 sc worked in ch), working in unused lps on opposite side of ch, sc in next ch and in each ch across to ch at base of first sc, 4 sc in next ch (place marker in first sc of 4 sc worked in ch): 214 sc. Do not join.

Rnd 2: [Work 2 sc in next sc, sc in each sc across to marked sc, 2 sc in marked sc, sc in next sc (place marker in this sc), 2 sc in next sc, sc in next sc] twice: 220 sc.

Rnd 3: Rep Rnd 2: 226 sc. Finish off, leaving a 12" (30.48 cm) tail for sewing.

Finishing
Wash and block bag. Allow to dry.

Assembly
Cut 3 lengths of clothesline for each handle (or fewer lengths if clothesline is thicker), approx. 2" (5.08 cm) shorter than length of handle. Apply fabric glue to end to prevent fraying and allow to dry. Lay clothesline at center on wrong side of handle and whipstitch long edges together, encasing clothesline and leaving 16 stitches at end of each handle free. With right sides facing, sew ends of handles in place on appropriate lt green sections near top of tote bag (see photo for handle placement).

MOSAIC CROCHET

[M]osaic Crochet is a fascinating technique of crochet [whi]ch utilizes 2 contrasting colors of yarn (usually a [ligh]t and a dark color) to "draw" vertical, horizontal [and] sometimes diagonal lines. The designs that can be [crea]ted with this technique are limitless. While there are [man]y methods of working Mosaic Crochet, here is one [of t]he most popular.

How To Do Mosaic Crochet

[In] Mosaic Crochet, rows of light and dark stitches are [wor]ked using only one color of yarn per row. Typically, [just] 2 rows of one color is worked before switching to [the] other color. In many mosaic projects with one row [wor]ked in each color, the ends will be turned into fringe [on b]oth side edges, eliminating the need to weave in 2 [end]s on each row. If the project has 2 rows worked in [eac]h color, the unused color is carried up the side edge [to b]e used again later and the carried strands are covered [by a]n edging, eliminating the need to weave in multiple [end]s again! Since only one color is used in each row, [ther]e is no need to change colors mid-row and the colors [don]'t get tangled, which often happens with changing [col]ors across a row.

[T]he horizontal lines of Mosaic Crochet are formed by [alte]rnating the rows of light and dark colors. The vertical [line]s are formed by working a taller stitch in front of the [pre]vious row (on the right side of the work) into the row [bel]ow the previous row (typically referred to as "one row [bel]ow" in the pattern). Diagonal lines are worked almost [the] same as vertical lines, but into a stitch in a row below [tha]t is "before" or "after" the current stitch location, [acc]ording to the pattern. These vertical and diagonal [line]s also add texture to the Mosaic project.

[T]o form the horizontal lines in our Mosaic Crochet [pro]ject, sc are worked into one loop of the stitches on [the] previous row: in the back loop on the right side [row]s and in the front loop on the wrong side rows. This [lea]ves the other loop of the stitches free to be worked [int]o when working the vertical stitches on the following [row]. To form the vertical lines in our Mosaic Crochet [pro]ject, an "anchored" st called an "anchored double [cro]chet" (abbreviated Adc) is worked. This one stitch [is w]orked in 2 places: in both loops of the stitch in the [pre]vious row and in the free loop of the stitch in the row [bel]ow the previous row (one row below). This anchored [stit]ch helps to keep the work from being loose on the [bac]k, especially in Mosaic Crochet designs where many

vertical stitches are worked in succession. The anchored dc covers up the horizontal line (on the right side of the work) that is formed in the previous row. Whenever a horizontal line is desired in a project, a vertical stitch (Adc) is not worked above it in the following row.

Anchored double crochet (Adc)

Step 1
Insert hook in both loops of specified st and draw up a lp: 2 lps now on hook.

Step 2
YO, insert hook in front lp of st one row below same st and draw up a lp: 4 lps now on hook.

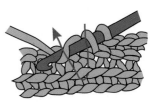

Note: *When inserting hook in front lp of st one row below, insert hook from top to bottom of loop, whether inserting hook on front of work (on right side rows) or on back of work (on wrong side rows).*

Step 3
YO and draw through 2 lps on hook: 3 lps rem on hook.

Step 4
YO and draw through all 3 lps on hook.

Completed anchored dc (Adc).

Note: *If the anchored dc is worked in a wrong side row, the hook will be inserted into the front loop of the stitch in the row below at the back of the work as it is facing you (on the right side of the work).*

Mosaic Basketweave Place Mat

Designed by Susan Lowman

for Red Heart®

nished Size: Approx. 13" x 19" (33.02 cm x 48.26
), including fringe

aterials:
rsted weight yarn 【4 Medium】
0% acrylic, 7 ounces, 364 yards (198 grams, 333
ters)] per skein
 skein blue
 skein yellow
 e I/9 (5.5 mm) crochet hook (or size required for gauge)
 te: *Photographed model made with Red Heart® Super
 er® #885 Delft Blue and #320 Cornmeal.*
 pestry needle

 uge: 14 sts = 4" (10 cm)
       14 rows = 4" (10 cm)

itch Guide

nchored double crochet (Adc): Insert hook in both
 ps of specified st and draw up a lp, YO, insert hook in
 nt lp of st one row below same st and draw up a lp, YO
 d draw through 2 lps on hook, YO and draw through all
 ps on hook: Adc made.

tes:

 ave a 4" (10 cm) tail for fringe at beginning and end of
 :h row.

 join at beginning of each row, make a slip knot and
 ce on hook. Work first st as usual.

 en working anchored dc on wrong side rows, insert
 ok in front lp of st one row below on back side of work
 right side).

structions

 aving a 4" (10 cm) tail, with blue, ch 59 loosely. Finish
 , leaving a 4" (10 cm) tail. Turn.

 w 1 (right side): Leaving a 4" (10 cm) tail, join blue
 th sc in back bar of last ch made, sc in back bar of each
 n ch across: 59 sc. Finish off, leaving a 4" (10 cm) tail.

 w 2: With wrong side facing, join yellow with sc in
 nt lp of first st, sc in front lp of each rem st across.
 nish off.

Row 3: With right side facing, join blue with Adc in first
st, sc in back lp of next st, Adc in next st, [sc in back lp of
next 5 sts, Adc in next st, sc in back lp of next st, Adc in
next st] 7 times: 16 Adc and 43 sc. Finish off.

Row 4: With wrong side facing, join yellow with sc in
front lp of first st, Adc in next st, [sc in front lp of next 7
sts, Adc in next st] 7 times, sc in front lp of last st: 8 Adc
and 51 sc. Finish off.

Row 5: With right side facing, join blue with Adc in first
st, [sc in back lp of next st, Adc in next st] 29 times: 30
Adc and 29 sc. Finish off.

Row 6: With wrong side facing, join yellow with sc in
front lp of first st, sc in front lp of next 4 sts, [Adc in next
st, sc in front lp of next 7 sts] 6 times, Adc in next st, sc in
front lp of last 5 sts: 7 Adc and 52 sc. Finish off.

Row 7: With right side facing, join blue with Adc in first
st, sc in back lp of next 3 sts, [*Adc in next st, sc in back
lp of next st, Adc in next st*, sc in back lp of next 5 sts]
6 times; rep from * to * once; sc in back lp of next 3 sts,
Adc in last st: 16 Adc and 43 sc. Finish off.

Row 8: Rep Row 6.

Row 9: Rep Row 5.

Row 10: Rep Row 4.

Rows 11 through 42: Rep Rows 3 through 10, 4 more
times.

Rows 43 through 45: Rep Rows 3 through 5.

Row 46: With right side facing, join blue with sl st in
back lp of first st, sl st in back lp of each rem st across:
59 sl sts. Finish off.

Finishing:
Matching row colors, add one strand of fringe to each
row on side edges of placemat, inserting tails into fringe
before tightening. At beginning and end of place mat,
make one blue fringe and insert both blue tails into fringe.
Trim fringe to 1" (2.54 cm), or to desired length.

GENERAL INSTRUCTIONS

Abbreviations and Symbols

Crochet patterns are written in a special shorthand which is used so that instructions don't take up too much space. They sometimes seem confusing, but once you learn them, you'll have no trouble following them.

These are abbreviations

Beg	begin (ning)
BL	back loop
BLO	back loop only
Ch (s)	chains
Cl(s)	Cluster(s)
Cm	centimeter
Cont	continue
Dc	double crochet
Dc dec	double crochet decrease
Dec	decrease
Dtr	double triple (treble) crochet
Edc	extended double crochet
Fig	figure
FL	front loop
Hdc	half double crochet
Inc	increase (ing)
Lp (s)	loop (s)
Mm	millimeter
Oz	ounces
Patt	pattern
PC	popcorn
Prev	previous
Rem	remaining
Rep	repeat (ing)
Rev	reverse
Rev sc	reverse single crochet
Rnd(s)	round (s)
Sc	single crochet
Sc dec	single crochet decrease
Sk	skip
Sl st	slip stitch
Sp (s)	space (s)
St (s)	stitch (es)
Tog	together
Tr	triple (treble) crochet
V-st	v-stitch
YO	yarn over hook

These are Standard Symbols

*An asterisk (or double asterisks**) in a pattern row indicates a portion o[f] instructions to be used more than once. For instance, "rep from * three tim[es]" means that after working the instructions once, you must work them agai[n] three times for a total of 4 times in all.

:The number of stitches after a colon tells you the number of stitches you have when you have completed the row or round.

( ) Parentheses or [ ] brackets enclose instructions which are to be worked [a] number of times following the parentheses or brackets. For instance, "(ch [1,] sc, ch 1) 3 times" means that you will chain 1, work one sc, and then chai[n] again three times for a total of six chains and three scs.

These are Standard Terms

Front Loop – This is the loop toward you at the top of the crochet stitch.

Back Loop – This is the loop away from you at the top of the crochet stit[ch.]

Post – This is the vertical part of the crochet stitch.

Finish Off – This means to end your piece by pulling the cut yarn end through the last loop remaining on the hook. This will prevent the work fr[om] unraveling.

Continue in pattern as established – This means to follow the pattern sti[tch] as it has been set up, working any increases or decreases in such a way tha[t] the pattern remains the same as it was established.

Work even – This means that the work is continued in the pattern as established without increasing or decreasing.

Crochet Terminology

The patterns in this book have been written using the crochet terminology [that] is used in the United States. Terms which may have different equivalents i[n] other parts of the world are listed below.

United States	International
Double crochet	treble crochet
Gauge	tension
Half double crochet	half treble crochet
Single crochet	double crochet
Skip	miss
Slip stitch	single crochet
Triple crochet	double treble crochet

FRINGE

Cut a piece of cardboard about 6" wide and half as long as required for strands, plus ½" for a trimming allowance. Wind the yarn loosely and evenly lengthw[ise] around the cardboard. When the card is filled, cut the yarn across one end. Do this several times; then begin fringing. Additional strands can be wound as the[y] are needed.

1. Hold the specified number of strands for one knot of fringe together and fold them in half.
2. With right side facing you, use a crochet hook to draw the folded ends through the space or stitch from right to wrong side.
3. Pull the loose ends through the folded section.
4. Draw the knot up firmly.

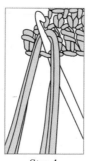
Step 1

Step 2

Step 3

Step 4